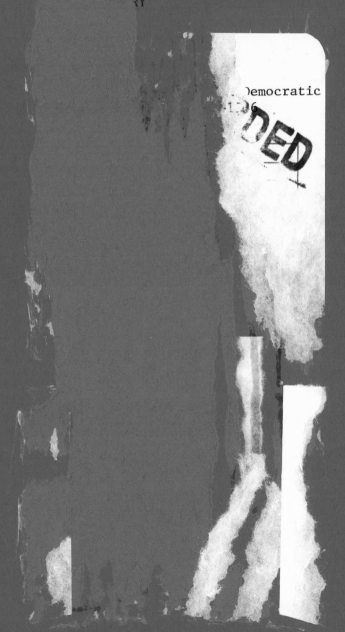

Democratic

The Creation of a Democratic Majority

1928–1936

The University of Chicago Press
Chicago and London

Kristi Andersen

The Creation of a
Democratic Majority
1928–1936

KRISTI ANDERSEN is assistant professor of political
science and associate director of the Polimetrics
Laboratory at the Ohio State University.

The University of Chicago Press, Chicago 60637
The University of Chicago Press, Ltd., London

© 1979 by The University of Chicago
All rights reserved. Published 1979
Printed in the United States of America

83 82 81 80 79   5 4 3 2 1

Library of Congress Cataloging in Publication Data

Andersen, Kristi.
    The creation of a Democratic majority, 1928–1936.

    A revision of the author's thesis, University of
Chicago.
    Bibliography: p.
    Includes index.
    1. Democratic Party—History. 2. United States—
Politics and government—1929–1933. 3. United States
—Politics and government—1933–1945. I. Title.
JK2317 1928.A53 1979   329′.3′09042 78-11660
ISBN 0-226-01884-9

Contents

v

Figures

Tables

Preface

Two articles in a recently published volume entitled *Political Opinion and Behavior* deal with the prospects for a partisan realignment in the 1970s (and the possibility that one has already occurred), but their conclusions are varied and somewhat equivocal.[1] The authors of both pieces hark back to the last major realignment that America experienced as a kind of baseline from which to discuss the possibility of future realignments. While they, and everyone else, agree that the years between 1928 and 1936 witnessed a significant change in the political agenda and in the parties articulating the issues on that agenda, in at least one sense they clearly have very different notions of *how*, exactly, that realignment took place. There has always been a vigorous debate about *when* the realignment happened—the elections of 1928, 1932, and 1936 vie with one another for the distinction of "critical election"

—but there appears as well, on close examination of the literature, a much more subtle and less clearly articulated disagreement about *how* the New Deal realignment occurred. Quotes from these two articles give a good idea of two possible perspectives:

> The parties took their stands at the respective poles of the argument. In that time of catastrophe, the New Dealers won. Millions of former Republican voters (most of whom had cast a protest vote for Roosevelt in 1932) shifted allegiance permanently to the Democratic party and converted it from the country's minority party to its power majority. [P. 335]

> . . . long-term Democratic gains came, not from the conversion of voters who had been in the electorate before 1929, but from new voters who reached voting age in the depression and post-depression years. [P. 138]

Sundquist, whose view is presented in much greater detail elsewhere,[2] expands upon the popular mythology of the New Deal realignment: Bad times caused Republicans by the millions to become Democrats. Sundquist, of course, presents a sophisticated and convincing analysis, describing where (in the northern cities) and when (it varied from place to place) this mass conversion took place, using detailed voting returns and registration figures. Many writers—scholarly and popular, historians and political scientists—have implicitly adopted a version of this popular mythology: by speaking of the "conversion" or "reshuffling" of voters, they leave the impression that aggregate change occurred through individual party-switching.

Other writers, however, Ladd among them, appear to subscribe to the idea of "mobilization," rather than "conversion," as the mechanism of change. Mobilization is the process whereby previously apolitical citizens are simultaneously pulled into the political arena and acquire a party identification. Through conversion, however, citizens who are already politically active (or at least voting) abandon their previous party identification and begin to identify with another party. Aside from Samuel Lubell, the authors of *The American Voter* were perhaps the earliest proponents of the mobilization position.[3] They pointed to a pro-Democratic swell among new voters around the time of the 1932 election and concluded that Roosevelt's support must have come largely from a new generation of voters whose Democratic identification persisted into the 1950s. This argument is made concisely in two pages; the authors had neither the data nor the inclination to develop it further. Yet it has been cited repeatedly as the last word on the source of the realignment; in fact, the statement from Ladd quoted above is immediately supported by a citation from this portion of *The American Voter*.

Thus, on the one hand, we have a seldom examined popular mythology and, on the other, passing and unquestioning references to a political science classic. The *mechanics* of the realignment have never been subjected to intensive study, and therefore neither point of view has been empirically verified. Yet because it is an event within memory, because it spawned the current partisan alignment, the New Deal realignment is usually the one we draw on for examples when discussing the general phenomenon of realignment. The fact that the essential individual-level dynamics that produced it have not been carefully sorted out leaves us with a tremendous gap in our knowledge of these events and of the process of partisan change in general, even though we take for granted our knowledge of it and our ability to generalize from this knowledge.

The mobilization of groups outside the core electorate, however, played a more important role than the conversion of loyal Republicans in creating the Democratic majority that emerged from the realignment. The popular mythology, as well as sophisticated refinements of it, fails to consider several factors, which, taken together, render conversion unnecessary, if not implausible, as the major explanation for the realignment. These factors include, first of all, the nonvoting element of the population. Much of the misunderstanding surrounding the dynamics of this realignment (and possibly others) stems from the unconscious assumption that change takes place in a fully mobilized electorate. This has never been the case in the United States, and most particularly it was not the case in the 1920s, when turnout rates in all elections fell to an all-time low. Not surprisingly, nonvoters were highly concentrated during this period in immigrant-stock areas of the northern cities. There is a second factor that must be considered: the growth during the years preceding the realignment of a sizeable group of new citizens, immigrants with no firm partisan loyalties and no psychic investment in any previous alignment. Finally, there is the factor of generational change. An unconscious assumption that often distorts the analysis of partisan change is that the composition of the electorate remains the same over time. This oversight prevents proper consideration of the impact of new generations on the distribution of partisan strength, and of the passing of older ones as well.

Nonvoting populations, immigration, and generational turnover are considered here as sources of a mobilizable mass which formed the basis of the new Democratic majority. Because of the inadequacy of the data available, it is impossible to conclude definitely—as we would be able to do were a realignment to occur tomorrow—about the precise relative impact of each of these factors.

The first chapter is concerned with the treatment of partisan realignment by American political scientists and particularly with the apparent inconsistency between the usual view of the stability of party identification on the one hand and the image of realignments as mass abandonment of party identification on the other. That the notion of potential and actual electorates whose rates of growth vary over time and according to political circumstances is essential to the study of realignment is the point of the second chapter.

In the third chapter the growth during the 1920s of a large pool of "nonimmunized" citizens—those without strong party identifications and with little experience of political participation—is described. The result of this is the subject of the following chapter. Here, questions from the 1952–72 Survey Research Center election studies were used to "reconstruct" the party identification of the electorate during the 1920s and 1930s and to clarify the role of the younger generation, many of whom entered the electorate in the twenties but failed to vote until 1928 or later. It has been argued that the markedly Democratic tendencies of this generation could only occur in the context of a massive rejection of parental partisan preferences. Chapter 5 shows that it is unnecessary to reject the

claims of socialization research if it is remembered that many
in the parental generation were nonvoters, immigrants, independents, and supporters of minor parties.

Up to this point, the arguments are based mostly on survey
data, largely retrospective (though some early Gallup polls are
also used). Partly because of the questionable nature of these
recall data and partly because of the desirability of focusing
more closely on an area which, among others, played a central role in the realignment, the sixth chapter uses various aggregate data in a case study of the realignment in Chicago.

This research was originally done for a dissertation in the
Department of Political Science at the University of Chicago.
The members of my dissertation committee, Norman Nie, Sidney
Verba, and Ben Page, were helpful and encouraging through-
out the several years of research and writing. I am also grate-
ful to Bill McAllister, John Petrocik, Steve Yarnell, John
Kessel, Herb Asher, Warren Miller, and Walter Dean Burn-
ham for various suggestions and criticisms.

One

American Politics, Political Science
and the Dynamics of Realignment

American political parties have historically been characterized by a certain fluidity of support, leadership, and policy. Historians have remarked less on the enduring characteristics of these organizations than on their apparent ability to transform themselves frequently and substantially. One example: in 1896 the urban working class played a significant role in the consolidation of the Republican-dominated "system of 1896"; a mere thirty years later, Democratic gains among precisely the same group prefigured the New Deal realignment.[1] This fluidity has given students of American parties a perspective that is quite different from that of their European counterparts. Parties in Europe can be seen, in general, as the expression of the most significant regional, religious, economic, or ethnic cleavages in a society. The historic connections of parties with particular groups in society have usually been treated more or less as givens, as have the relative strengths of the parties, since they are based on the relative significance of the social segments.[2] Partisan change or realignment (as it is discussed by American historians and political scientists) is thus of less interest than the original development of the cleavages

1

that the now "frozen" party alternatives reflect. In contrast, the American parties' ability to behave "pragmatically" in attracting the support of diverse groups, as well as the existence of modern parties in the United States during the whole of the country's history, results in a scholarly emphasis on large-scale changes in the party system that is distinctly American.

Critical Elections as the Basis of Partisan Change

The first and most notable attempt to describe and classify elections in terms of their role in producing lasting changes in the partisan landscape was that of V. O. Key. He asserted that certain elections in American history, which he termed "critical elections," constituted an "election type" in which "the depth and intensity of electoral involvement are high, in which more or less profound readjustments occur in the relation of power within the community, and in which new and durable electoral groupings are formed."[3] For example, Key uses election returns by towns to describe the emergence of a new alignment in New England in 1928. The immigrant, urban, and Catholic were suddenly pitted against the native, rural, and Protestant, an alignment that persisted for at least twenty years. The election of 1896 was marked by a similar drastic change in party fortunes, though in this case the alignments generated proved to be less urban-rural or class than sectional.

Key's most important successor as an analyst of critical elections is Walter Dean Burnham. Burnham's concerns are somewhat broader than Key's: he tries to develop a general theory of the relationship between politics and the socioeconomic environment, in which critical elections act periodically to restore the two to a semblance of synchrony.[4] Thus he begins where Key leaves off: he demonstrates briefly the existence of critical elections and goes on to analyze their causes and their effects on politics (e.g., "depoliticization" of the electorate after 1896). The data Burnham brings to bear are varied. They range from national and state voting data and national turnout figures used to demonstrate the periodicity of critical realignments, to county returns and census data for a more detailed look at realignments in Pennsylvania.

James Sundquist offers an historically more comprehensive view of the processes of change that have characterized the American party system. Through the use of a vast array of election returns at all levels, he studies not only the New Deal and 1896 realignments, but the period of the birth of the Republican party in the 1850s as well. His aim is

in each case to identify the forces that disturbed the stability of the existing party system, to trace their origin and development, to examine the behavior of the parties in response to them, and to follow the events of the crisis to its ultimate resolution in the establishment of a new and once again stable party system.[5]

In Sundquist's view, critical realignments take place when new issues cut across existing lines of party cleavage and polarize the political community in a new way. The result can be the destruction of one party and the birth of a new one (1856), the absorption of a third party by one of the older parties (1896), or the realignment within the old parties of the policy positions and bases of support to take the new, polarizing issue into account (1930s).

Many other historians and political scientists, of course, have seized upon the concept of critical elections as a way to analyze partisan change systematically. MacRae and Meldrum, for example, analyzed critical elections in Illinois by means of principal component analysis.[6] Clubb and Allen tried to disprove the claim that 1928 was a critical election in the cities, finding that Democratic strength (as measured by vote for Congress and other subpresidential offices) in urban areas was on the upswing throughout the 1920s.[7] And a study by Shover, which applies Key's methods to California, finds that the Democratic gains of the early thirties were "part of a voting cycle which has been established earlier"; 1928 was not a critical election in California.[8]

Critical Election Theory and
Partisan Conversion

Despite the differences in theoretical frameworks, in the substantive political events being discussed, and in methodology, all of these studies share a certain perspective on the dynamics of partisan change.[9] The dependence of critical election studies on aggregate voting data has generally either obscured the role of the individual citizens in partisan change or has produced certain assumptions about the behavior of individuals in times of change. In turn, these assumptions support a particular notion of how partisan change happens, and that notion has direct implications for a theory of American party politics.

More specifically, critical election theory, at base, assumes that partisan change occurs when large numbers of individuals decide, at a particular time, to change their habitual patterns of voting. A crisis atmosphere attends such large-scale repatterning. Indeed the political crisis, the "grievance," the "tensions" that "escalate to a flash point"[10] are the reasons for the sudden alteration of political cleavages, which constitute a critical realignment. In voting in a critical election, people express their grievances through the party system. The picture drawn of a high intensity, high salience, polarized politics leads one almost inevitably to consider individual partisan "conversion" as the basis of realignment.

In Key's study of New England as well as in Burnham's study of Pennsylvania, sharp changes in the habitual electoral behavior of citizens are more or less taken for granted. Key speaks of "the great reshuffling of voters" that occurred in 1928, of "a large-scale transfer of party affection," which is, in critical elections, "broad and durable."[11] Burnham is a little more precise: "large blocks of the active electorate—minorities, to be sure, but perhaps involving as much as a fifth to a third of the voters—shift their partisan allegiance."[12] It must be admitted that in general both Key and Burnham ignore the issue of the actual behavior of individual voters in critical realignments. They speak of counties, towns, or states as moving in a particu-

lar partisan direction, "deviating," "defecting," or most important, "converting"; the notion of individual conversion is merely
implied. Burnham does, however, go beyond this, and he makes
the assumption of individual change in behavior more than
implicit when he criticizes the model of voting behavior implicit in the Survey Research Center work.

> Realigning elections are clearly qualitatively different from
> the norm of American electoral politics; . . . these funda-
> mental qualitative differences also suggest that models of
> voting behavior derived from the normal inertial stability of
> a mass middle-class identified electorate, which usually has
> no great perceived personal stake in the outcome, may fall
> short of describing the total potentialities of the American
> voter when abnormal circumstances politicize him.[13]

The survey-based "Michigan model" of the voter and voting
behavior must certainly be taken into account—even if it is to
be successfully modified by critics such as Burnham—by any-
one attempting to understand the dynamics of partisan change.
Paramount in this model is the importance of party identification—a sense of psychological attachment—in determining the
individual citizen's political attitudes and (especially) voting
behavior. "The role of general partisan orientations in molding
attitudes toward the elements of politics is very clear."[14] Recognition of and attitude toward political issues and candidates,
in turn, determine one's vote. More important for the analysis
of partisan change at the aggregate level are two other attributes of party attachment. The model views party identification
as largely "inherited." It has been shown to be transmitted in-
tergenerationally with far higher frequency than other political
attitudes.[15] And this inherited predisposition is stable and enduring: "identification with political parties, once established,
is an attachment which is not easily changed."[16]
    If individuals' partisan identifications are stable, how then
does a redistribution of party support happen? One way of re-
conciling the notion of enduring party attachment with the fact
of sharp partisan change has been adopted by many of those

interested in critical elections and realignment. The picture of most voters as almost irretrievably tied to a party is accepted, with the important caveat that at times of extraordinary political upheaval old habits are broken and even these voters are moved to discard old party attachments in favor of new ones. The slavery issue in the 1850s, the depression of 1893 and the threat of agrarian radicalism posed by Bryan, the crash of 1929, and the Great Depression are universally conceded to have been events capable of producing such conversions.

Burnham's previously quoted statement indicates that this is the path he has taken; Sundquist seems to have accepted even more completely the survey-based findings that most individuals maintain a deep and stable attachment to a political party. It is important to recognize that Sundquist's notion of conversion, which is fundamental to his theory of realignment, applies not only to voting behavior but to "what underlies voting behavior —to the basic party attachments of the voting citizens."[17] Partisan change can, of course, occur in other, more gradual ways. Sundquist calls this type "inorganic" change in the party system. New groups are enfranchised, one party may benefit from different birth rates, or individuals for personal reasons may convert to the other party (e.g., Democrats moving to the suburbs may become Republicans). These types of movements are relatively unimportant, however, in Sundquist's understanding of the history of the American party system. In contrast, during the periods of "organic" change—the 1850s, 1890s, and 1930s —"the existing rationale for the division of voters between the parties gave way to a new one. One or both of the major parties was radically changed in composition and character." The party structure was, in effect, shifted on its axis by the decisions of innumerable individuals to change their party affiliation.[18]

At first glance the authors of *The American Voter* seem to have opted for this approach. Despite the stability of individual party identification found to characterize the electorate in the 1950s, it is admitted that "occasional cataclysmic national events have had the power to produce substantial realignment in long-standing divisions of political sentiment."[19] But they are of two minds about this. In speaking specifically of the New Deal realignment, they say,

There can be little doubt that some of the new Democrats were old Republicans. There is reason to believe, however, that a good many of these Republicans who defected into the Democratic ranks during the early years of the Roosevelt period were soon disenchanted. Some erstwhile Republicans never returned to their party, but these party-changers do not appear to have made up a very large part of the Democratic increase. Our inquiries into the political histories of our respondents lead us to believe that a larger component of the gain came from younger voters entering the electorate and older people who had previously failed to vote.[20]

In a recent article, Philip Converse has expanded substantially on this idea. "It is easy," he says, "to sketch a model of what was going on in this period which requires a proportion of true conversions scarcely more than a percentage or two of the electorate as a whole."[21] Instead, reminding us of the constant turnover of the national electorate, Converse suggests that the rapid change in the partisan coloration of the electorate between 1928 and 1940 can be accounted for almost wholly by Democratic recruitment of young voters in that period. Thus the brief treatment in *The American Voter* and Converse's lengthier discussion raise the possibility that indeed the stability and centrality of party identification can in some historical periods be reconciled with the fact of measurable, rapid change in the partisanship of particular social groups and in the relative strength of the parties nationally.

The Importance of Mobilization in Electoral Change

The notions that major partisan realignment necessitates widespread individual conversion and that conversion can only occur in a crisis atmosphere sometimes present problems of analysis. The most persistent problem of this type is the election of 1928, the "critical" nature of which has been extensively debated.[22] Despite the distinctly new appeal of Al Smith, 1928 can hardly be described as a political "earthquake." Nonetheless, that conversion was the heart of the change in party alignment that occurred in 1928, particularly in the cities, is not questioned. Rather, say Clubb and Allen in an investigation of this election,

> Large-scale changes in party affiliation and habits of electoral participation have been rare and have been identified with times of major national crisis. If realignment came in 1928 as a result of developments less dramatic than national crisis, it may be necessary to modify views of the stability and intensity with which partisan loyalties have been held.[23]

Such a solution is both unsatisfactory and unnecessary. Instead, I will argue that processes which can be collectively labelled "electoral replacement" were more significant than conversion in accounting for the partisan change that took place in the late twenties and early thirties. The groundwork for this theory is laid by Key's sometimes overlooked article on secular realignment. Less dramatic processes than those which bring about critical elections, says Key, "operate inexorably, and almost imperceptibly, election after election, to form new party alignments and to build new party groupings." An occupational, religious, or geographic grouping "becomes either more or less homogeneous in its partisan attachment. A variety of factors operates over time either to solidify the group or to erode the ties that unite it politically."[24] An "objective change in the status of a group" is, Key speculates, the most likely basis for this type of long-term change, but he does not dwell on the dynamics of the change.

How does a group composed of individual citizens change, over time, from one which is perhaps 50 percent Democratic to one which is 80 percent Democratic? It is certainly true that such change is the sum of individual decisions, but such a process is too narrowly conceived if the "decision" can only involve changing from a Democratic to a Republican affiliation or vice versa. An independent or nonaffiliated voter can make a decision to "become" a Democrat or a Republican. In each election, all voters must make the decision to participate or not. One may make a decision at the point of entering the electorate to adopt or reject the party of one's parents. These individual decisions are being made all the time; their concentration at particular periods or around particular events determines the speed and direction of partisan change.

Several people have suggested that the 1928–36 realignment was based more on "mobilization decisions" than on "conversion decisions." One of the most convincing is Samuel Lubell. He argues that the "Roosevelt revolution," as well as what might be called the "Al Smith revolution," was the result of the influx of immigrants to United States cities in the early part of the century and the coming of age of their children twenty to thirty years later.[25] In a more recent and more systematic analysis, Carl Degler shows that in cities with 50 percent or more immigrant stock, the Democratic vote increased enormously from 1920 to 1928, while the Republican vote increased substantially less. Smith mobilized the immigrants and their children as no one else had been able to do.

> Some of these voters of immigrant stock had probably been voting Republican all along and now switched to the Democrats. But many more, it would seem, voted for the first time, for otherwise one cannot explain the enormous increase in Democratic votes without a commensurate decline in Republican votes.[26]

Immigrant women, in particular, who had received the franchise in 1920 but had failed to vote then or in 1924, suddenly turned out in 1928 to support Smith. In precincts within heavily Italian census tracts in Boston, for example, female registration rose by nearly 30 percent in 1928.[27]

This type of movement may be "inorganic change," as Sundquist would argue, but it is not definitionally so. Conversion decisions are not the only manifestations of a change in the "existing rationale for the division of parties and voters." In this case, the Democratic party, beginning in 1928, changed its basis of support largely by appealing to hitherto politically uninvolved groups such as women, young people, and the foreign-stock, urban, working class. Roosevelt and the Democrats, says Lubell, "awaken[ed] the climbing urban masses to a consciousness of the power in their numbers. He extended to them the warning hand of recognition, through patronage and protective legislation."[28] And as a result, the policies and the composition of both parties were substantially altered.

Why Conversion Has Been a More Popular Explanation than Mobilization

Why has the possibility of this type of change often been overlooked by political scientists and historians? First, election returns (which, by default, have formed the basis of the analysis of realignments) are most commonly analyzed by asking how the percentage of Democratic or Republican votes in a particular area varies over time. This method can obscure important facts: it does not normally take into account either changes in turnout or changes in the size of the eligible electorate. Thus conversion is the "natural" interpretation when a city or county, say, gives 60 percent of its vote to the Republicans in one election and 60 percent to the Democrats in a subsequent election. In turn, the assumption that permanent conversion from one party to another is always the cause of significant partisan change encourages the view that a single political event or crisis is behind it all. The introduction of the concept of party identification was not necessary to establish the idea of switching from one party to another as serious business which could only happen on rare occasions— occasions characterized by a crisis atmosphere. The primacy of conversion as a means of partisan change has been further solidified by the general if implicit assumption of full mobilization. Though some observers, particularly Burnham, are concerned with rates of turnout, high levels of participation have usually been viewed as outcomes rather than causes of realignments. Further, many of those who have taken increased turnout into account, especially in explaining the New Deal realignment, have failed to consider as another independent variable the increasing size of the potential electorate.

Second, the idea of voters deliberately discarding party loyalties in times of political change has an appeal for those who would like to be convinced of the "rationality" of the American voter. If the model of the "irrational," essentially uninvolved but highly partisan voter is accepted, the notion of the classical

"good citizen" can be redeemed only by the idea that extraordinary political crises can change political behavior (in this
case, can cause people to change their party attachments). The
ideal-typical voter implied in Sundquist's "scenarios," for example, moves to support whichever party is seen to represent
most of (or the most important of) his or her interests, once
the rationale for party division has changed.

Key argues that the prevalence of voter rationality over the
short term (from one election to the next) is supported by the
connections between issue positions (for example, in 1936–40,
favorable attitudes toward the Social Security or farm relief
programs) and vote-switching (in this case, from a Republican
to a Democratic vote). "Standpatters," in contrast, tend to ad-
here to the "pure and orthodox . . . tenets of their party; thus
their consistency in voting from one election to the next can
also be considered 'rational.' "[29] More recent studies of "issue
voting," though not concerned specifically with switchers and
standpatters, as was Key, also suggest the influence of policy
attitudes on the electoral decision.[30] Which voters are moti-
vated to vote which way by which issues will, of course, always
be a central inquiry of political science. But debate about the
short-term rationality (however that is defined) of the individual voter, while it can be illuminating and even fundamental
to the study of long-term, permanent partisan changes in the
electorate, should not be allowed to suggest that conversion
(i.e., "switching," not of one's vote but of one's enduring party
loyalties) is the only means by which "rational" voters can
precipitate a realignment.[31]

The point is that a theory of change which places emphasis
upon electoral replacement and mobilization of new voters,
while it does not have to be a sociologically deterministic one,
is bound to consider "rationality" in a different and more general way than studies of election-specific "issue voting." Policy voting, whether in the context of particular salient issues
or general liberal or conservative orientations, can be seen as
an issue of defection versus party voting. Party identification,
however, is more resistant to change, and it is this "lagging
indicator" with which we are primarily concerned in discussing
realignment. Arthur Goldberg has demonstrated the "ration-

ality" involved in adopting or rejecting parental party identification, a "rationality" defined not by attitudes on specific
issues but by very generally perceived group interests.[32] Gerald
Pomper has made a similar point:

> In many electoral analyses, issues are considered only as
> short-term influences, distinct in their effect from partisan
> loyalty. . . . This assumption is analytically convenient, but
> it underestimates the long-term effects of issues. One of the
> sources of party identification itself is policy attitude, and
> attitudes first evident in one election may continue to be
> relevant and influential in succeeding contests.[33]

Affective feelings toward or general evaluations of a party,
then, which form the basis for the voter's psychological identification with that party, may originate in an acceptance of
parental preferences or in a rejection that brings party identification into line with policy positions. After this, however, the
general evaluation—for example, Democrats are, or were in a
remembered instance, better for the working man—persists in
its significance. At the same time secondary processes, such as
group norms, organizational and personal ties to local party
organizations, and so on, operate to reinforce the original positive evaluation. Those who base their behavior on such long-
term evaluations, as Pomper warns, should not be considered
"unthinking prisoners of tradition and habit."

A demonstration that conversion is less important than it
has been thought to be, therefore, does not mean that we must
abandon "rationality" (or the more satisfactory concept of rea-
sonableness) as a framework for viewing the voter. It is em-
phatically *not* the case that, as Charles Sellers maintains, such
a demonstration would be "a shattering refutation of any theory
that sees ideology, issues or direct perception of interest as a
primary determinant of voting behavior."[34] On the contrary,
the alternative process of change—based on the mobilization of
"nonimmunized" populations—involves decisions that are as
apt to be "rational" (i.e., based on evaluations of the electoral
alternatives in terms of preferred policy outcomes) as are conversion decisions.

Political Immunization
and Partisan Change

The concept of political immunization has been used by McPhee and subsequently by others to refer to the notion that political experience—usually in the form of voting—establishes and reinforces one's commitment to the democratic electoral system and to a particular party. Those who have voted more often, regardless of their age, are less likely to be affected by short-term political stimuli. The greatest source of political instability for an established party system, in this view, is the arrival of new individuals who have little experience or sympathy with the divisions of that party system.

One possible source of such new and uncommitted members of a political system is the extension of the franchise. Early in the history of democratic polities changes abolishing land-owning qualifications and other financial considerations as criteria for suffrage increased the size of potential electorates enormously, as did, at a later date, the extension of the franchise to women. Subsequent legal modifications in electoral laws have acted to expand (or contract) the electorate in subtler ways: registration and voting are made compulsory or more difficult; literacy tests and poll taxes are introduced; ballots are made simpler or more complex.[35] In the United States, identifying changes (whether of size or behavior) in the electorate that are the result of institutional changes is vastly complicated by the prerogatives of the individual states in establishing election laws. Elimination of property requirements, for example, proceeded state by state between 1790 and the Civil War, by which time white male suffrage was the rule almost everywhere.[36]

The other major changes in the composition of the (potential) United States electorate have been the fifteenth and nineteenth amendments and the series of court decisions in the 1950s and 1960s which effectively reenfranchised southern blacks. In all such cases of franchise extension, the new citizens are nonimmunized: while they may enter the system with a partisan preference, their lack of political experience means their partisan commitment is lower—and their potential political volatility greater—than that of other citizens.

A nation's citizenry can also be rapidly and disproportionately swelled by immigration—an even more obvious case of the system having to cope with a large number of people not yet socialized to its values and not yet committed to its partisan divisions.[37] It has been suggested that the successive waves of immigrants to American shores played an important role in McKinley's defeat of Bryan in 1896 and in the New Deal realignment.[38] Richard Jensen's study brings out what is perhaps the most significant point about immigrants in this context: in a society where political loyalty is (or was) quasi-religious in nature, immigrants enjoy a relative freedom from the constraints of party attachments.[39]

Of course new citizens are constantly entering the electorate —each year thousands of young people attain their majority— but this process generally does not produce marked or rapid partisan change. Though the coincidence of the eighteen-year-old vote and the 1972 campaign generated speculation about the sudden impact of a new generation on the election results, the failure of youthful left-wing unanimity to materialize seemed to confirm the notion that the passage of generations is a form of continuity rather than a cause of change. Indeed, a strong and consistent finding is the extent to which partisan loyalties are handed down from parents to children.[40] The partisan political socialization provided by one's parents and reinforced by one's subsequent associations as an adult is seen as ensuring the intergenerational continuity of partisan divisions by providing new citizens with what might be termed "preimmunization."

Generally, failure to adopt parental party identification has been explained in terms of individual psychosocial characteristics, such as social mobility or aspirations to social mobility, family child-rearing practices, and so forth.[41] Even Goldberg, who argues convincingly that both adherence to and defection from parental preferences can often be viewed as "rational," fails to consider outside political events or changes in the political universe as variables that might affect intergenerational transmission of party identification. Surely there are situations where the central issues of politics have altered substantially over a period of time and where the party coalitions may therefore be coming apart. Here the turnover between generations can

be expected to accelerate partisan change, in contrast to more
placid times, when "inherited party loyalties are a powerful
anchor dragging against . . . social change."[42]
The issues that give birth to a particular partisan alignment
inevitably fade with the passing of time. In 1965, 35 percent
of the high school seniors questioned in a national survey could
not identify Franklin D. Roosevelt's party.[43] Several recent
studies have indicated that the "traditional" (i.e., since the
1930s) class basis of the Democratic-Republican split is less
important among younger voters.[44] Some have even shown a
tendency for the class-party relationship to reverse itself altogether among the newest generation.[45] Theoretically, this
process can happen very slowly, and over a period of generations the social bases of the parties may be altered completely
as a new set of issues gradually replaces the old. More likely,
new polarizing forces will arise more rapidly. As Butler and
Stokes describe it, "strong new primary forces can sweep away
political attachments that depend mainly on the intrinsic values [psychic or social utilities] of party."[46] And since younger,
less experienced voters are more politically flexible, less fixed
in their attitudes, their partisan habits and preferences are far
more likely to be affected by the new forces than are those of
older citizens. This is precisely the "organic change" that Sundquist is talking about. Given the reluctance of individuals to
abandon long-held partisan attachments, however, it stands to
reason that changes in the "existing rationale for the division
of voters"[47]—changes in the kinds of issues emphasized and
choices presented by the parties—would naturally have their
greatest impact on the behavior and attitudes of the newest political generations. Or, to state this proposition in terms of the
arguments advanced by E. E. Schattschneider, the irrelevance
of old conflicts and the appeal of alternative organizations of
conflict will be recognized most easily by new voters.[48]

Finally, if the basis of "immunization" is "political experience," a variable-sized group of nonimmunized citizens will
exist in any political system not characterized by full mobilization. The United States is, and has been during most of the
twentieth century, a system with an enormous number of habitual nonvoters.[49] The theoretical potential for sudden change in

such a situation is dramatically described by Schattschneider: "we are governed by invisible forces, for to an astonishing extent the sixty million [voters] are at the mercy of the rest of the nation which could swamp all existing political alignments if it chose to do so. The whole balance of power could be overturned by a massive invasion of the political system."[50]

Has something like this ever happened? All the critical election theorists note the rise in participation that accompanies a period of realignment. Key, for example, characterizes critical elections as times when "voters are . . . unusually deeply concerned, [and] in which the extent of electoral participation is relatively quite high."[51] "High intensity" and "heavy voter participation are terms also used by Burnham to describe critical elections.[52]

It is clear from these statements that both authors (and they are by no means unique) view the volume of participation and the new bases of party support as two independent phenomena, both caused by the rise of new, polarizing issues. In the specific context of the 1930s many historians and political scientists have recognized the advantage Democrats gained from the mobilization of immigrant groups, but a solid theoretical connection between realignment and the mobilization of nonparticipants has not been made.

The reason for this failure has to do with the way in which nonvoting has traditionally been viewed by American political scientists. Beginning in 1924, when Merriam and Gosnell accounted for all the nonvoters they studied by "general indifference and inertia," "physical difficulties," "legal and administrative obstacles," and "disbelief in women's voting or disgust with politics,"[53] personal and psychosocial deficiencies have been seen as the major impediments to voting. "It is often a mistake," say the authors of Voting, "to give purely political explanations for nonparticipation."[54] One might argue that it is equally mistaken to give a purely nonpolitical explanation (e.g., "persistent social conditions") for nonvoting.[55] In fact it is surprising that although nonvoters are often described as having many social and economic characteristics in common (e.g., lack of income and education), they are not assumed to have political interests distinct from the rest of the population—an assumption which is routinely made about groups of voters who share certain socioeconomic attributes. The shortsightedness of the major survey-based studies of voting in this regard is obvious. While it is true that their respondents may not give explicitly "political" (i.e., election-connected) reasons for failing to vote—seeming instead to project a general disinterest—if the cleavages that are at present represented in American politics do not speak to their interests, then a vote loses its value, and their nonvoting, while not consciously political, has political implications of the profoundest sort. Schattschneider states this argument clearly: "Abstention represents the suppression of the options and alternatives that reflect the needs of the nonparticipants."[56] In general, though of course not in all specific cases, nonvoters begin to vote not merely because they have become "more interested" in politics but because the political agenda has changed and new, more attractive choices appear to be offered to them.

If turnout is explained primarily by psychological factors, the intense political atmosphere generated by new issues may cause heightened interest among those previously uninterested and, therefore, a higher voting rate. At the same time, the new issues are forming the bases for a new alignment of partisan forces through an exchange of supporters by the parties. The two processes are independent outcomes of the growth of new issues, since those who are mobilized to participate are not assumed to have a distinct set of interests. By extension, although by virtue of their political marginality they may tend to jump on bandwagons, their conscious collective choice of one party or the other is not a foregone conclusion.

If, however, turnout is mostly a function of the choices offered and the extent to which those choices make voting worthwhile for people with different interests, the rise of new issues may expand the scope of political conflict to include new segments of the public. The "organic change" in the rationale of the partisan cleavage thus will have a direct impact on turnout, by bringing these new voters into the system. In turn, the mobilization of new groups by one party or the other, as opposed to conversion of people already in the active electorate, forms the basis for a realignment of partisan forces.

In summary, it is argued here that the role of the nonimmunized—whether immigrants, new voters, or those who for some
reason have abstained from voting—in the New Deal realignment (and by extension in all realignments) should be considered much more seriously than scholars have done heretofore. Not only did those without strong party identifications in
the prealignment period form a group large enough to change
the partisan balance, but by the nature of things the nonimmunized were so located in the population that they were particularly responsive to the articulation of a new cleavage and new
issues.

Two

Expansion of the Electorate and Partisan Change

The failure to see the importance of changes in the voting turnout and in the size of the electorate is among the factors behind the acceptance of conversion over mobilization as an explanation of partisan change. Increases in political participation have frequently been mentioned as a *consequence* of critical elections, of course. Burnham, for example, says critical elections are characterized by "abnormally high intensity," one aspect of which is "abnormally heavy voter participation for the time."[1] Key and Sundquist also include increases in turnout as a result, if not a defining characteristic, of critical realignments. But turnout per se is not a primary concern of either of these two authors.

Burnham, in contrast, is intensely concerned about the implications of decreases in turnout and other evidence of party decomposition. But he examines the relationship between the size of the actual electorate and realignment on the assumption that the latter is always the independent variable. The election of 1896—or more properly the party system that resulted from it —is shown to have depressed participation and increased volatile and erratic behavior on the part of the electorate. But neither increases in the size of the electorate nor mobilization of particular groups in the electorate is thought of as having helped produce the realignment of 1896 or, for that matter, the New Deal realignment.[2]

The New Deal realignment is unique, as far as I know, in that it has raised the possibility that change in turnout can be viewed as an independent variable, realignment as the dependent variable.[3] But generalization from the particular experience of the 1920s and 1930s to an explanation of partisan change taking into account the role of newly mobilized populations has not been forthcoming. In general, "realignment theory," loosely defined, has not taken seriously the physical expansion of either the actual or potential electorate as factors in partisan change.

Nonimmunization and New Issues

By itself, electoral expansion cannot be considered a "cause" of realignment. But rapid expansion of the electorate increases the possibility that a large nonimmunized population will develop. At the same time, the expansion of the electorate is likely to mean that new divisive issues will arise. Since the emergence of new issues that can shatter old alignments and the availability of a population with few strong ties to the old alignments are both necessary before large-scale, permanent partisan change can take place, the connections between electoral expansion, new issues, and nonimmunization are worth examining.

Expansion of the Potential Electorate

The distinction between rapid expansion of the potential electorate and rapid expansion of the actual electorate is important in this context. Let us consider the former. Rapid increases in the number of people eligible to participate in national elections have come about, in the United States, in three ways. (1) New states have been admitted, driving up the number of eligible voters. For example, Minnesota, Oregon, Kansas, West Virginia, Nevada, and Nebraska were admitted to the

Union in the eighteen years preceding the 1876 election; the result was that about 8 percent of the potential electorate in that year resided in newly admitted states. (2) Constitutional amendments and other changes in the electoral laws can produce a surge in the number of eligible voters. The most dramatic expansion of this kind came with the passage of the nineteenth amendment proclaiming women's right to vote. An expansion somewhat less dramatic numerically occurred with the ratification of the fifteenth amendment prohibiting states from denying Negroes the right to vote. (3) At several periods in American history the adult population, and therefore the potential electorate, has been swelled especially rapidly by immigration. The immigration rate (number of immigrants per 1000 population) peaked in 1851–60, when the rate was 9.3, again in 1881–90, when it was 9.2, and in 1901–10, when it was 10.4[4]

In all of these cases, the electorate expands by *groups*. In contrast to the kind of electoral expansion that goes on constantly as citizens come of age, this type of expansion takes in categories of people who by definition are different from the rest of the electorate. In the first case, that of territorial expansion, they are people who have chosen a new way of life which, it can be argued, generates economic interests different from those of the more established areas. In the second and third instances, the additions to the electorate are composed of classes of people who have previously been excluded from the system (women, blacks, the nonpropertied), or people entirely new to the system (immigrants). It is reasonable to assume that rapid expansion of the electorate by any of these means—particularly changes in electoral laws or immigration—may well add to the electorate people who have a set of common interests that differ from those of the rest of the electorate. Historically this has been most true of immigrants, whose needs and problems are bound to be quite different. In the United States, later immigrants in particular arrived and settled in large groups, immediately facing problems of housing, job discrimination, poverty, and slum conditions.

Another requisite of partisan change or realignment—a large pool of nonimmunized citizens—most obviously results from expansion through immigration. A half million to a million potential voters—adults whose formative political experiences took place in other, often very different, kinds of political cultures—disembarked in this country every year between 1890 and 1910. The elements of political socialization that make for stable and predictable electoral behavior, that is, the early inculcation of party loyalty and repeated experiences of voting for one party, require lengthy exposure to the political culture and to socializing agents such as schools, unions, and other associations, or big-city political machines. Because of the psychological resistance involved in accepting new ways of behaving politically, in fact, the social learning process by which party loyalty is progressively acquired and reinforced may be more prolonged for, say, a thirty-five-year-old immigrant than for a twenty-one-year-old new—but native—citizen.[5]

Electoral expansion by territorial accretion is a less extreme but possibly still significant way in which the nonimmunized population can grow rapidly. "It can be shown that temporal variation in party voting and ticket splitting—both supposed to be symptoms of weakly developed partisanship in aggregates— are remarkably high in the 'new voting systems' represented in American states freshly admitted to the union in the late nineteenth and early twentieth centuries."[6] Similarly, fragmentary data indicate that newly enfranchised women in Chicago were more likely to split their tickets and to vote for third parties than were their male counterparts with a longer experience of voting.[7]

Expansion of the Actual Electorate

While the result of rapid growth in the *potential* electorate, through immigration, extension of the franchise, or territorial expansion can bring about or speed up the rise of new political issues, the expansion of the actual electorate can always be largely explained by issues. Put simply, people vote or do not vote because of what they perceive the political stakes to be. E. E. Schattschneider is probably the most eloquent exponent of this theory. Even if his argument is not completely accepted, it would seem that the roots of what might be described as purely "psychological" noninvolvement in politics or "disinterest" must have something to do with the perceived ir-relevance of current politics.

In a two-party system that at any given point is based on only a limited number of political cleavages or conflicts, poli-tics is quite likely to be thought irrelevant by many people.[8] If the nature of the central political argument changes, if the lines of cleavage are redrawn, different people (if not more people) will be moved to participate in the system. Now if this hap-pened with some regularity—say, from election to election—even though characterized by a low turnout rate, the system still would not be burdened with a large group of nonimmu-nized citizens, because different groups with different interests would be voting in each election. This hypothetical situation is some distance from reality. The major lines of political cleav-age (what politics is about) change only infrequently, and the American political system is characterized at the present time, at least, by a large mass of habitual nonvoters. In 1972, for ex-ample, nearly 30 percent of those eligible said they never voted or voted only sometimes, as opposed to always or most of the time, in presidential elections; the question of whether or not they have voted produces a notorious overstatement of turnout.

The coincidence of the rise of new issues with the existence of a large pool of nonimmunized citizens is the raw material of realignment. If the expansion of the *actual* electorate as con-flicts are altered or become more intense consists largely of those people who have been the basis for recent growth in the *potential* electorate, the possibilities of lasting realignment are increased tremendously. In other words, previous changes in the composition of the electorate (voters and nonvoters) will de-termine the significance of an increase in turnout for partisan change. Immigrants or newly enfranchised voters, without es-tablished partisan loyalties or patterns of political behavior, are more open to mobilization by one party or the other on the basis of these new issues. A similar political volatility or open-ness may or may not characterize nonvoters who are suddenly mobilized to participate by an issue or a candidate. I will argue later that in the realignment of the 1920s and 1930s, this was true of the nonparticipants partly because they shared some crucial characteristics with the new voters.

Measuring Electoral Expansion

Burnham has shown that changes in the level of turnout in presidential elections are related to the periodic realignments that are suggested by his voting data. But this relationship is far from perfect—the turnout series, says Burnham, show only very broad processes at work, for example, the "massive process of turnout decline associated with the 'system of 1896' " and the "remobilization of the mass electorate" subsequent to the New Deal realignment.[9] Turnout levels per se, however, are less interesting than the two components of turnout discussed above: expansion (or contraction) of the actual electorate and of the potential electorate. If important shifts in the electoral fortunes of the parties are largely a result of their success at recruiting previously nonvoting groups, then major realignments may be expected to take place during periods of rapid expansion of the actual electorate. In this case we should look for increases in the number of votes cast, instead of increases in turnout (the proportion of those eligible who vote). Further, we should look at the relationship between changes in the number of votes cast and changes in the size (and composition) of the potential electorate. An increase in the proportion of citizens voting can have an unambiguous meaning—mobilization of people who did not vote in the previous election—only if the population base remains constant. This has, of course, never been the case; it is important to know the source of additions to the potential electorate and when and how these additions are incorporated into the actual electorate.

A straightforward examination of the votes cast in each presidential election since 1848 reveals a clear association between growth in the actual electorate and periods of partisan change. Discounting the increase in votes cast between 1864 and 1868 as a response to the Civil War, the highest percentage increases came in the following election years: 1856, 1876, 1896, 1916, 1920, 1928, 1936, and 1952. The three periods generally associated with critical realignments (the elections of 1856, 1896, 1928, and 1936) are prominent in this list, as are several other elections, which could be said to have produced "minor" realignments. Eighteen seventy-six saw the establishment of Democratic ascendancy in the South and, perhaps, the conclusion of the realignment that had begun twenty years earlier.[10] In 1916 there was again something of a regrouping of Democratic forces after a period of Republican dominance. The dramatic increase (43 percent) in votes cast between 1916 and 1920 represents, of course, the extension of the franchise to women.

Short-term surges in the size of the voting population, then, do seem to be associated with periods of partisan change. But the existence of such a pattern by itself says nothing about whether these surges are the cause or the result of realignments. If we want to make distinctions among the circumstances producing rapid increases in the number of votes cast for a president, it is necessary to explore the relationship between changes in the actual electorate and changes in the potential electorate. Neither the turnout rate nor the rate of increase in votes cast takes the changes in the population base into account.

Figure 1 presents a ratio of the increase in the actual electorate from one election to the next to the increase in the potential electorate during the same period.[11] A ratio of one indicates that changes in the size of the actual and of the potential electorate are proceeding apace. This can occur under either of two conditions: In the first, large additions to the population (through immigration or territorial expansion, for example) are counterbalanced by a political system able to engage new citizens as they enter the electorate. Even though the population is expanding, turnout does not decline; the condition of nonimmunization does not become widespread. In the second situation, slow or "normal" growth in both the actual and the potential electorate means that the citizenry is being enlarged mainly through natural growth in the population and that new generations of citizens are being adequately socialized in terms of party loyalty and the desire for political participation.

A ratio below one means that the potential electorate is growing faster than the voting population. It is in this situation that large numbers of nonimmunized citizens, citizens who have little experience with politics and fragile loyalty to a particular party, are most apt to develop. There will be a greater incidence of nonimmunization if the people represented by the gap be-

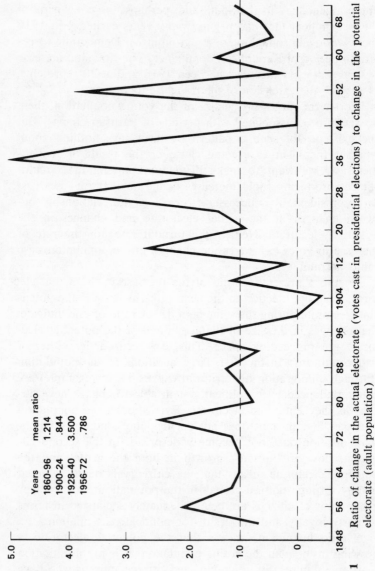

Years	mean ratio
1860-96	1.214
1900-24	.844
1928-40	3.500
1956-72	.786

Figure 1

Ratio of change in the actual electorate (votes cast in presidential elections) to change in the potential electorate (adult population) tween the potential electorate and the actual electorate are *habitual* nonvoters. Theoretically, nonoverlapping groups can choose to sit out succeeding elections. But, given the major sources of rapid increases in the potential electorate—extension of the franchise, immigration, the granting of statehood—it is reasonable to assume that rapid population growth, without a commensurate increase in the actual electorate, will produce a substantial group of nonimmunized nonvoters.

Finally, if the ratio in figure 1 is above one, the increase in the electorate is outstripping the growth of the population. Some sort of voter mobilization is taking place. Whether this represents only a heightening of interest among an electorate already participating or a sudden integration of new voters into the system depends on whether a pool of nonimmunized voters has been created by the politics of the preceding years. In figure 1, the peaks (when mobilization was more rapid than population growth) are similar to those found in the examination of the increase in votes cast, and the overall pattern fits nicely the descriptions of sequential "party systems" offered by Ladd, Burnham, Sundquist, and others. In the post-Civil War party system, between 1860 and 1896, the mean ratio of increase in the actual electorate to increase in the potential electorate is 1.21. This accords with Burnham's picture of the electorate in the late nineteenth century as being effectively mobilized by the parties and highly active, at least in terms of voting.[12] The subsequent "system of 1896," in contrast, shows a mean ratio of only .84, indicating that during the period between the realignment of 1896 and the New Deal realignment, the population was growing faster than the vote. More data must be examined before we can talk about the extent to which the nonvoters of this period constituted a growing pool of nonimmunized citizens who contributed significantly to the realignment to come. The political era encompassing the 1928 election and the New Deal years was a period of dramatic mobilization, indicated by the fact that on the average, the percentage increase from year to year in the vote was 3.5 times greater than the yearly percentage increase in the potential electorate. Finally, it is interesting to note that the sixteen years between 1956 and 1972 appear very similar to the "system of 1896" in terms of the system's apparent inability to mobilize voters and the consequent growth of a large pool of nonimmunized citizens.

Electoral Expansion and the Vote

When the electorate expands quickly, the benefits usually accrue to only one of the parties. Thus from 1872 to 1876 the Republicans gained only 400,000 votes, while the Democratic vote totals increased by nearly 1.5 million. In 1916 Wilson received almost 3,000,000 more votes than he had gotten four years earlier, while Hughes gained only about 900,000 over the combined 1912 totals of Roosevelt and Taft. This lopsided effect is not always found: the increase in votes cast (and in turnout) in the election of 1928, for example, went to both Democrats and Republicans. The political circumstances surrounding a particular election may determine who profits in such a situation, but even more significant is the sociodemographic and political complexion of the upsurge in votes. The increase in the Republican vote between 1924 and 1928 probably came mostly from Republicans who had not voted in 1924 or from anti-Smith Democrats (especially Southerners) temporarily deserting their party. In other words, this expansion of the Republican electorate was not a stable base upon which to build a new and lasting coalition. Smith's candidacy, however, greatly increased the participation of the urban working class and immigrant groups whose continued Democratic partisanship was essential to the building of the New Deal majority.[13]

The dramatic nature of the realignment that took place in the late 1920s and early 1930s is easily described with voting data. The change in Democratic fortunes was abrupt. In a few elections, the situation changed from one in which pundits were speculating about the party's impending disappearance (in 1920 and 1924 the party received only 35 percent of the two-party presidential vote) to one in which the Democrats enjoyed undisputed legislative and executive hegemony. Their share of the vote increased rapidly, to 59 percent in 1932 and to 62 percent in 1936. If over this twelve- or sixteen-year period the population—the potential electorate—had remained static, and if there had been full or nearly full participation during this period, such a change could only have been accomplished by a massive conversion of large numbers of Republicans to the opposition. But neither of those conditions held. Turnout increased from about 43 or 44 percent of the voting-age population in 1920 and 1924 to about 57 percent in the Roosevelt-Landon election of 1936. More important, between 1920 and 1936 the total number of votes cast for president increased by 70 percent; thus about 40 percent of the 1936 electorate was new since 1920.

Moreover, a casual inspection (see fig. 2) of the numbers of votes cast in presidential elections in the twenties and thirties

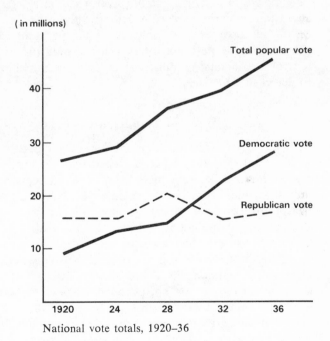

Figure 2   National vote totals, 1920–36

(rather than the percentage of the vote obtained by each party) gives some credibility to the notion that these new votes went predominantly to the Democrats. The most striking thing about this figure is the stability of the Republican vote. In 1920 Hard-ing received 16,333,314 votes; in 1936 the Landon vote was 16,679,543. Except for the upsurge in the Hoover-Smith election (as noted above, the increase in votes from 1924 to 1928 benefitted both parties), the Republican vote in the five elections from 1920 to 1936 remained remarkably constant, even though the Republican share of the two-party vote dropped from 64 percent in 1920 to a low point of 38 percent in 1936. In contrast, while only 9,140,884 voters went to the polls for Democrat James M. Cox in 1920, Roosevelt received 27,757,333 votes sixteen years later—more than the total number of votes cast in the 1920 election! The Democratic vote more than tripled.

Although this exercise should serve to plant a seed of doubt about the significance of conversion on the New Deal realignment and serve as a warning about the perils of looking at the vote only in percentage terms, it can only suggest the pattern of Democratic mobilization of new voters, which I hope to depict in more detail.

Were Northern Republicans Converted?

"The millions who switched parties between 1928 and 1936, and stayed switched, can be identified most readily by place of residence. They were concentrated in the industrial cities of the North."[14] Cities like New York, Chicago, Detroit, Milwaukee, Pittsburgh, and Philadelphia had large working class populations and were the destination of most of the late nineteenth- and early twentieth-century immigrants to the U.S. They were the essential building blocks in the new Democratic coalition, but exactly how they came to vote consistently Democratic (or more strongly Democratic than before) is open to question. Sundquist is the most adamant and the most convincing proponent of the "conversion" hypothesis. He uses voting data and information about partisan registration from various types of communities to demonstrate his point that the basis of the realignment consisted of Republican-to-Democratic conversions among the Northern urban working class.[15] A brief reanalysis of voting and registration data sim-

ilar or identical to Sundquist's may, however, point tentatively
to the significance of new voters in the realignment (see chap.
6 for a more detailed treatment).

Table 1 presents the Republican vote and the total votes cast
in presidential elections between 1920 and 1936 for seven
northern urban counties. The table also includes the change
(increases, with two exceptions) in the Republican vote from

Table 1   Votes Cast and Republican Votes in Seven Urban
                   Counties, 1920–36 (in thousands)

County	1920	1924	1928	1932	1936	Percent Change, 1920–24, 1932–36
New Haven						
Total	109.5	120.5	165.0	174.1	204.6	+ 64.6
Republican	65.9	69.2	80.9	79.9	76.6	+ 15.8
Cook (Chicago)						
Total	893.1	1133.7	1540.2	1664.2	2009.5	+ 81.2
Republican	635.2	689.0	812.1	690.1	701.2	+ 5.0
Wayne (Detroit)						
Total	295.0	335.3	426.7	543.6	626.1	+ 85.6
Republican	220.5	268.6	265.9	212.7	190.7	− 17.5
New York						
Total	464.4	463.3	521.6	565.2	711.3	+ 37.6
Republican	275.0	190.9	186.4	378.1	174.3	+ 15.1
Cuyahoga (Cleveland)						
Total	231.3	264.1	364.1	370.6	475.4	+ 70.8
Republican	148.9	130.2	194.5	166.3	128.9	+ 5.8
Allegheny (Pittsburgh)						
Total	200.7	253.0	379.2	359.0	562.2	+103.0
Republican	138.9	149.3	215.6	152.3	176.2	+ 14.0
Philadelphia						
Total	142.3	148.0	206.2	259.4	297.0	+ 91.7
Republican	73.4	50.7	82.0	54.7	54.8	− 11.8

1920–24 to 1932–36 (an average of the two years' votes in each case) and a similar measure of the expansion of the voting population.[16]

These are the areas where, by some accounts, large-scale shifts from the Republican party to the Democratic party should have taken place. The urban workers who had rejected Bryan's agrarian radicalism in 1896 and paved the way for three decades of Republican domination had suddenly—thanks to Al Smith and the Depression—been brought into the Democratic fold. Or so the argument goes. But, as the figures in table 1 show clearly, there was in these cities virtually no decline in the Republican vote from 1920 to 1936. There are local variations: in New York, for example, already a Democratic city in the early twenties, the expansion of the electorate is less dramatic than it is elsewhere and there is greater variation in the Republican vote. In Philadelphia the Republican vote declined a bit over the sixteen years. Generally, though, the actual electorate in these cities grew by 50–100 percent, while the Republican vote totals increased only 5–15 percent. There was a similar trend in cities with a high proportion of immigrant stock between 1924 and 1928. In nineteen cities with over 50 percent immigrant stock, the Democratic vote increase averaged 205 percent; the average Republican increase was 29 percent; only three cities showed an absolute decline in the Republican vote total during these eight years. This is a very important point: even in the immigrant-stock cities, there was no appreciable decline in the Republican vote totals. Equally significant is the contrast between ethnic and native cities with regard to the expansion of their electorates. The actual electorate (total votes cast) in Degler's "ethnic" cities grew by 73 percent between 1920 and 1936, that of the nonethnic cities by only 28 percent, even though many of the latter cities were expanding substantially in population.[17]

While it is unwise to draw inferences about individual behavior from patterns such as these, the smaller the unit of analysis the more confidently we can speculate about the individuals constituting them. While on the national level the pattern of a stable Republican vote coupled with a massive increase in the vote could mask a multitude of partisan exchanges among different regional, class, ethnic, or other groups, this is not quite so true of data at the county level. The counties in table 1 are more or less homogeneous demographically: in 1936, as in 1920, they were highly industrialized and disproportionately foreign stock and working class. Even though it is possible that Republican recruitment of young middle-class voters or independents and disaffected Democrats in these urban counties was sufficient to offset the hypothesized mass conversion to the Democrats, the persistence of the pattern we have found casts substantial doubt on this theory. So does what we know about voting behavior, of course: as Angus Campbell reminds us, "when the political tide is running against a party, it reduces that party to its loyal partisans; the party will lose most of the support it may have received at other times from Independent voters or from defectors from the other party."[18]

Changes in Party
Registration Figures

To supplement his review of changing voter patterns, Sundquist uses data on party registration or enrollment.

Registration is a positive act by a voter to identify with a party as such, as distinct from giving his support to the party's candidate in a particular election. For purposes of analyzing party alignment, therefore, registration data have the great advantage of ignoring the deviant voting behavior that so frequently confuses the interpretation of election returns.[19]

In terms of assessing gradual changes in party loyalties, registration data, despite their liabilities, can be considered the "next best thing" to survey data.

There is no question that the information Sundquist presents —the Democratic percentage of two-party registration in selected counties in New York, Pennsylvania, West Virginia, Oregon, and California—shows a "massive realignment" in the early 1930s. As the percentages make clear, the Democrats went from a distinct minority to a majority of the party registrants in many of these locales, especially the Northern urban counties. Further, the registration data indicate that the realignment occurred at different times in different places and that some areas, for example, in upstate New York and in the Pennsylvania Dutch counties, were nearly unaffected by the Democratic trend.

But to infer from these data that the realignment was based on massive switching of party affiliations would be unwarranted. These are the conclusions Sundquist draws, and they are cited by Converse as proof that there were, indeed, many "converts" during this period. "The shift of voters in the registration books was sudden, decisive, and permanent. . . . In the metropolis of Allegheny County (Pittsburgh), the proportion of Democratic voters rose between 1930 and 1938 from 7 percent to 58 percent—a shift equivalent to more than half the county's voters."[20]

This statement is not valid unless one can be certain that the number of voters remains constant or relatively constant. Actually, as will be seen below, the number of citizens registered to vote in Allegheny County increased by 67 percent in those eight years. In 1938 there were as many Democrats registered in the county as there had been voters of both parties registered in 1930.

Figures 3 through 8 are concerned with the changes in the patterns of voter registration in New York City, Albany, Philadelphia, and Pittsburgh and, by way of contrast, in two rural upstate New York counties. These figures are based on the same data as Sundquist's depiction of the change in the percent of Democratic registrants in these areas, but the numbers reveal more than the percentages about the dynamics of the realignment. For example, the percentages of two-party registration in New York City and Albany are closely parallel. In New York the Democrats claimed 66 or 67 percent of the electorate in the mid twenties, a figure which rose to 82 percent by 1936. Similarly, in Albany the Democrats constituted about 45 percent of those registered in the mid twenties, and 71 percent in 1932. But figs. 3 and 5 illustrate the significant variations to be found beneath the apparent parallel.

To begin with, the two counties differ greatly in the extent to which the registered electorate expanded. The growth in the number of people registered to vote was 64 percent in New

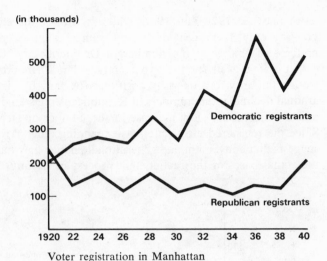

Figure 3   Voter registration in Manhattan

Source   *Manual for the Use of the Legislature of the State of New York* and *The Pennsylvania Manual* for the appropriate years.

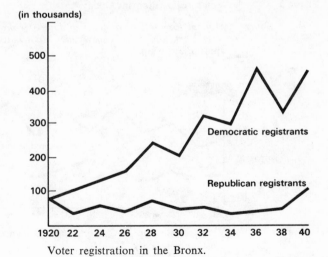

Figure 4   Voter registration in the Bronx.

Source   *Manual for the Use of the Legislature of the State of New York* and *The Pennsylvania Manual* for the appropriate years.

York between 1920 and 1936, while in Albany the electorate grew by only 32 percent during the same period. Second, the patterns of change in the number of Democrats and Republicans differ as well for the two counties. The Democrats went from a minority to a majority position in Albany by virtue of a gradual decline in the numbers of Republicans registered to vote and a concomitant slow increase in the number of Democrats. Since the registered electorate was expanding quite slowly, this suggests that conversion and generational change may have been the actual bases of the realignment process in Albany. In New

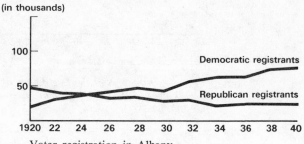

Figure 5   Voter registration in Albany

Source   *Manual for the Use of the Legislature of the State of New York* and *The Pennsylvania Manual* for the appropriate years.

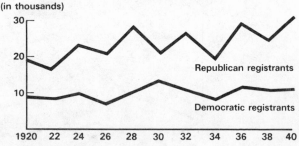

Figure 6   Voter registration in Chenango and Otsego counties (upstate New York)

Source   *Manual for the Use of the Legislature of the State of New York* and *The Pennsylvania Manual* for the appropriate years.

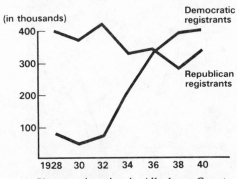

Figure 7   Voter registration in Allegheny County

Source   *Manual for the Use of the Legislature of the State of New York* and *The Pennsylvania Manual* for the appropriate years.

York, by contrast, the stability of the Republican portion of the registered electorate and the tremendous increase in Democrats (registered Democrats roughly doubled from the early twenties to the late thirties) suggest that the mobilization of new voters played a much more important role in the urban setting of New York. The same pattern is repeated—in fact, exaggerated—in the Bronx (fig. 4). In the similarly urban and immigrant-stock counties of Philadelphia and Allegheny, there is a somewhat steeper decline in the number of Republicans registered, but the most striking thing in figures 7 and 8 is the dramatic growth in registered Democrats in both cities. In these cases, of course, the changes bring the Democrats from a distinct minority to a competitive position, while in New York and the Bronx the Democrats' majority position of the early twenties was greatly strengthened by the realignment. In the two rural upstate counties of Chenango and Otsego, as in Albany, there is little expansion of the electorate compared with the urban counties. What growth there is benefits the Republicans. As Sundquist says, the realignment appears to have bypassed such areas.

From these data it appears, very simply, that a realignment occurred in places where the actual electorate expanded a good deal in the late 1920s and early 1930s. In the Bronx, those on

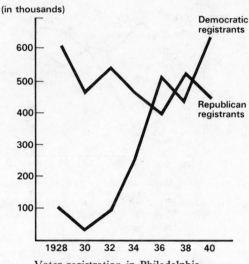

Figure 8   Voter registration in Philadelphia

Source   *Manual for the Use of the Legislature of the State of New York* and *The Pennsylvania Manual* for the appropriate years.

the voting lists in 1936 represented a 162 percent increase over the enrollees in 1924. In Manhattan there was an increase of 60 percent. In contrast Chenango and Otsego counties, where the relative strength of Democrats and Republicans remained fairly constant, the enrolled electorate grew by only 19 percent from 1924 to 1936. The massive expansion of the electorate in New York City was not due to a commensurate growth of the population during this time: Manhattan's population actually declined between 1920 and 1930, and there is no reason to believe that trend was reversed between 1930 and 1936. Rather, this seems to be a good example of the phenomenon of the mobilization of the nonimmunized: in the years before and during the realignment, expansion of the enrolled electorate in the urban counties of New York drew upon people who were already members of the *potential* electorate but who had not previously registered to vote.

Three

The Growth of a Nonimmunized Population

The twenties, like the early seventies, were years characterized by political disaffection and minimal citizen participation in politics. Walter Lippman, writing in 1927 on the causes of political indifference, attributed voter apathy partly to corruption and partly to prosperity and the "New Capitalism," but more importantly to the irrelevance of the current party alignments to the issues of greatest public concern and to the more or less deliberate efforts of party leaders to dampen public interest and keep new and conflictual issues from erupting.[1]

The Composition of the Nonimmunized Population

The rate at which eligible citizens voted, even in presidential elections, reached an all-time low in the early 1920s. Nationally, less than 45 percent of the eligible voters participated in the presidential elections of 1920 and 1924: turnout rates were about 55 percent in the North and 20–25 percent in the South.[2]

Much of this remarkably low turnout can be attributed to the passage of the nineteenth amendment: Women were slow to take advantage of their right to vote and this lowered the aggregate voting rates. Illinois gave partial suffrage to women in 1915, and breakdowns of voting behavior by sex are available for that period. Burnham estimates that sex differentials in turnout in Chicago and environs in the presidential elections of 1920 and the mayoral elections of 1915 and 1919 ranged between 20 and 30 percent. The difference between the sexes was greater in the city itself than in the better-educated, wealthier suburban areas.[3] Foreign-stock women especially did not enter too quickly the male preserve of politics. Merriam and Gosnell, in their 1924 study of nonvoting in Chicago, report that

> The women voted in relatively larger numbers in those wards where rental values were the highest and where the proportion of foreign-born was the lowest. From this it may be said that an unduly large proportion of the non-voting adult citizens were women of foreign extraction living in the poorest residential sections of the city.[4]

Furthermore, even those women who did begin voting in the early 1920s would have been less strongly committed to a particular party (if one accepts the "immunization" argument) than their male counterparts, who had been voting for years. Goldstein finds that women recently granted the franchise in Illinois were less stable in their voting behavior than men. In a relatively low-salience election such as that for the trustees of the University of Illinois the frequency of ticket-splitting was higher for women than for men, as was the drop-off rate (failure to vote a complete ticket). Again in the trustees' election, women were more likely to vote for third-party candidates: 21 percent voted for a Progressive party candidate, while only 16 percent of the men did so.[5]

A second factor contributing to the large pool of citizens available for mobilization was immigration. The wave of southern and eastern European immigrants crested in the first two decades of the century, but it has been estimated that the process of naturalization took an average of ten to twelve years. Thus many of those immigrants who did become United States citizens did so in the 1920s. In fact, census figures show that nearly twice as many people were naturalized in the decade 1920–29 as in the previous decade. It is worth noting that the four-year period that saw the most naturalizations was the period prior to the election of 1928.

Moreover, the children of the 1890–1910 immigrants were coming of age during this period. The fertility rates of foreign-born women in the early part of the century were significantly higher than the rates for native women. This is clearly manifested by the demographic "bulge" in 15–24 year olds of foreign or mixed parentage in the decade between 1920 and 1930 (see table 2).

Table 2   Percent Change in Population: Immigrants and Children of Immigrants, 1890–1940

| | | Foreign-born | | Foreign or mixed parentage | |
Period		15–24	25–44	0–14	15–24
1890–1900		3.0	17.9	25.0	13.9
1900–1910		42.1	33.2	7.7	21.5
1910–20		—30.9	6.7	17.4	4.7
1920–30		—22.7	— 6.2	— 8.9	**26.3**
1930–40		—66.7	—41.5	—42.7	— 6.7

Source   I. B. Taeuber and C. Taeuber, *People of the U.S.* (Washington: Bureau of the Census, 1971), p. 116.

Lubell describes the results vividly:

> In the winter of 1910 Congress received the longest report ever submitted by a government investigating body up to that time. From early 1907 a special commission had been studying almost every imaginable aspect of immigration . . . [it] showed that a majority of the children in the schools of thirty-seven of our leading cities had foreign-born fathers. In cities like Chelsea, Fall River, New Bedford, Duluth, New York and Chicago more than *two out of every three* children were the sons and daughters of immigrants. Viewed in today's perspective, it is clear that those figures forecast a major political upheaval some time between 1930 and 1940.[6]

In our terminology, these people were doubly nonimmunized, for they had no personal political experience and had not "inherited" a party identification from their immigrant parents. It is hardly surprising that the immigrants and even their children did not immediately enter wholeheartedly into the political process. Aside from the language barrier and the difficulty of attaining citizenship, the lack of connections with or stake in politics surely depressed the voting turnout of foreign-stock Americans.[7] And again, as with women, one would expect the party loyalty of even those foreign-stock citizens who did vote to be less stable, on the whole, than that of their neighbors whose roots went further back into the American political past.

In Pittsburgh, to take one example, presidential turnout in eight wards of poor foreign stock averaged only 36 percent during the twenties, while the average turnout during the same period in four wards of wealthy native stock was 45 percent.[8] In the Merriam and Gosnell study of voting and nonvoting in the Chicago mayoralty election of 1923, "occasional" nonvoters, those who were indifferent to the particular election, were likely to be found in native white wards, while "foreign birth and the female sex were closely related to habitual non-voting."[9] An examination of voter registration figures for 1925 makes it clear that the percentage of foreign-stock inhabitants is strongly related to low levels of voter registration. Applying a rough measure of registration levels (voters registered in February 1925 over estimated population in January 1925) to a map of Chicago wards in the twenties, one finds that the wards with the highest levels of registration are, almost without exception, located on the outer fringes of the city. They tend to be disproportionately native-born and relatively wealthy: 38 percent of the wards with over 45 percent of their inhabitants registered are among the ten "most native" wards; none are among the wards with the highest foreign-stock population. Conversely, those wards with less than 25 percent of their population registered to vote consist almost entirely of inner-city, new-immigrant neighborhoods. The 31st ward, for example, where registered voters were only 15.5 percent of the total population, was a predominantly Polish ward with among the lowest average rents in the city.[10]

Generational Change
and the Collective Memory

Another process, always at work, is the process of forgetting. The issues and coalitional loyalties that characterize a particular alignment of forces or a particular "party system" are most real to those people who personally experienced the formation of that alignment, and most liable to be acted upon by them. Younger people or recent immigrants may feel strong attachments to their preferred party, but these attachments, as the last period of party realignment recedes into history, are increasingly based on secondary forces. Sundquist aptly describes this process:

> For many people the emotional attachment to one party and the hostility toward the other formed at a time of crisis remain an essential part of their personal identities for the rest of their lives. To abandon one's party would be as unthinkable as to abandon one's country or convert to another church. For a powerful issue to fade, then, is in part a generational process, as new voters too young to have identified with either side at the time of polarization displace their elders.[11]

As he points out, one generation may not be enough to erase the images of conflict and the passions that regenerated party loyalties among the older generation, for these passions and loyalties are passed on to the new generation and experienced vicariously. In a recent article, Paul Beck examines more systematically these assumptions about generational change and realignment. He identifies three different groups in terms of the learning of partisanship. Members of a so-called realignment generation "adopt their enduring partisan orientations as emerging adult participants in a realigning phase." To their children this first group transmits a strong party preference: "No other generation will transmit partisan orientations as successfully to its offspring as this realignment generation." These groups, once their partisanship has been acquired and reinforced, will be relatively unsusceptible to forces encouraging partisan change. Instead, it is the newest members of the electorate (the "children of normalcy," in Beck's terms), who provide "the dynamic element in American electoral politics." Neither these people nor their parents acquired their partisanship during a period of political polarization, and their partisanship is therefore weak (or perhaps nonexistent) and subject to change.[12]

The question, then, is whether younger citizens during the prerealignment period of the twenties constituted a disengaged or nonimmunized population. Following Beck's method of locating political generations, one finds that those people who were young adults in at least the latter part of the decade can be considered "children of normalcy," and as such open to the influence of realigning forces. Assuming a 25 year age differential between parents and children, most (though not all) of the parents of those who experienced their formative years in the 1920s were too young to have participated in the realignment of 1896. Beck fails to consider the role of immigration, although doing so would strengthen the "generational" argument in this particular case. In 1930 fully 30 percent of the 18–30 year olds had at least one foreign-born parent. Most of them were children produced by the wave of immigrants that crested around 1900; most of their parents probably did not strongly identify with either party, and those who did have a party preference did not acquire it during the heat of the 1896 realignment.

More concrete evidence for the extent of nonimmunization among young voters would be data on the number of independents or the number of nonvoters in various age groups. In a period of political calm, we can expect a moderate relationship between age and partisanship. This pattern was found repeatedly, for example, in studies of the U.S. population conducted in the 1950s and early 1960s. The proportion independent decreased from about 30 percent to about 15 percent as one moved from the youngest age groups to the oldest.[13] In a recent study, Inglehart and Hochstein identify this as representing the " 'normal' age-partisanship slope under equilibrium conditions."[14] If it is true that younger citizens are more responsive to new events than older voters (and mountains of evidence lead us to believe it is), then one could expect them to be most affected by conditions producing rapid alignment or dealignment of the electorate—to be, in fact, the major contributors to such change. Inglehart and Hochstein find that during the first decade of the French Fifth Republic, a period of rapid alignment, the age-partisanship slope was flattened, if not reversed slightly.[15] And data from a Gallup poll conducted in March 1937, just at the end of the period of alignment that commenced in 1928, show a remarkably similar pattern. The difference between the youngest and oldest age groups in table 3, 4.8 percentage points, is very small compared with the difference found between similar age groups in the 1950s.

Table 3   Percent "Independent" or Having "No Opinion" on Their Partisanship, by Age Groups, 1937

Age	Percentage	Age	Percentage
21–24[a]	20.1	45–49	20.1
25–29	18.0	50–54	12.2
30–34	18.9	55–59	17.3
35–39	20.1	60–64	14.7
40–45	16.5	65+[a]	15.3

Source   Gallup Poll, March 1938, American Institute of Public Opinion #72; data supplied by the Roper Center.

[a]The difference between the oldest and youngest groups is 4.8%.

In periods of *dealignment*, such as the twenties, the late sixties, and the early seventies, Inglehart and Hochstein argue that the age-partisanship slope will be greatly exaggerated. They show that such a pattern existed in the United States in 1968; it has persisted since then.[16] Was there an equally strong relationship between age and partisanship in the decade preceding the New Deal realignment? Without survey data on party identification, we have no sure way of knowing.[17] The solution to this problem is to regard nonvoting, for the moment at least, as the functional equivalent of nonidentification with a party. Party identification, though acquired early in life, in order to be durable and impervious to short-term forces needs to be continually reinforced by voting. Particularly in the case of young people, failing to vote on attaining majority can be regarded as representing a low level of partisanship.

Thus in order to derive a rough estimate of the age-partisan-ship slope, one can compare the extent to which young citizens voted with the turnout level for the country as a whole. In fig-ure 9 the percentages of "first voters" reporting a vote in the presidential elections of 1924 and 1936 are compared with the levels of turnout among the whole population in the same years.

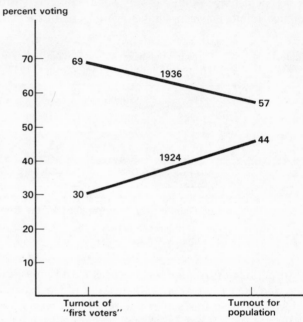

Figure 9   Alignment and dealignment

Source   For turnout of first voters, recall data on when respondent first voted (from Survey Research Center 1952 study), as described more fully in chap. 4; for turnout of the population, presidential votes cast in a particular year were divided by the estimated eligible population (citizens over 21).

The "dealignment" slope is not as steep as we might have expected: turnout was low among all age groups, not merely the young (and it should be noted that the figures reported here are only approximations). But the contrast in the age-partisan-

ship (or age-turnout) slopes between 1924 and 1936 is striking
and supports the view that the transition from the dealignment
period of the twenties to the realignment period of the thirties
was characterized by a marked shift in the political behavior of
the youngest groups in the adult population.

Additional evidence on the political disengagement of the
young in the decade preceding realignment can be gleaned
from sources such as Merriam and Gosnell. They found a
slight tendency for habitual nonvoters to be concentrated
among the young: while 28 percent of the registered voters
were between 21 and 29, 34 percent of the habitual nonvoters
fell in that age group. The age-nonvoting relationship varied
according to sex (older women, of course, made up a goodly
portion of the nonvoters) and nationality (among the older
immigrant groups, Irish, German, and Scandinavian, there was
a tendency for nonvoting to increase with age). But, in general, they note that "youthfulness was a factor which correlated
highly with complete lack of voting experience. About twice as
many of the habitual male nonvoters were in their twenties as
compared to the registered male voters."[18]

Finally, in 1925 in a study of voters and nonvoters in Dela-
ware, Ohio, it was found that people in their twenties were substantially less likely to have voted in the 1924 national election
than any other age group except those over 70.[19]

Party Politics and the
Fading of Alignments

Extension of the franchise, immigration, and
generational effects explain some, but not all, of the decline in
political participation witnessed in the 1920s. There are other
factors that must also be taken into account to understand the
prealignment period of the twenties and the dynamics of the
later Democratic surge; these factors have less to do with demography and more to do with politics.

Though partisan realignment can be thought of as being
composed of innumerable individual decisions, the reasons for
reevaluating longstanding political decisions have to do with
larger societal forces. Perhaps the most coherent description

of the sociopolitical disjunctions that may lead to realignment is that of Burnham:

> realignments are themselves constituent acts: they arise from emergent tensions in society which, not adequately controlled by the organization or outputs of party politics as usual, escalate to a flash point; they are issue-oriented phenomena, centrally associated with these tensions and more or less leading to revolutionary adjustments.[20]

Later in his book Burnham expands on this: socioeconomic development has been allowed to proceed in a largely unregulated, unfettered way in the United States, and because of this there have been periods when resources and benefits were allocated especially unequally. Since the political system is not characterized by similar developmental change, coalitions are re-formed in a relatively abrupt way when particular segments of society come to view themselves as disadvantaged or not represented in the current electoral and policy-making institutions.[21] To restate this process in the terms Schattschneider uses, groups that are politically "left out" succeed in changing the dominant political conflict. "The number of the subordinated conflicts in any political system must always be great. Every cleavage works to the disadvantage of millions of people. All those whose claims have been subordinated have an interest in a new alignment."[22]

But if these "restless elements," as Schattschneider calls them, are unable to redraw the lines of battle, if the central argument remains irrelevant to their interests, the result is, logically enough, their withdrawal from politics. The irrelevance of the conflict to them means that their votes are meaningless. The further away the political cleavages are from reflecting the most important social and economic interests in the society, the higher will be the level of nonparticipation.

A similar conclusion is reached with more theoretical elegance and more precision by political scientists concerned specifically with the rationality of voting and nonvoting. At least two types of party evaluation can lead a "rational" citizen to abstain from voting. These are, first, a situation in which the perceived difference between the two parties is so small that it does not outweigh the cost of the act of voting;[23] and second, a situation in which the parties may appear to be very different but both alternatives are unacceptable. Brody and Page suggest that the decision to abstain in the latter case can be considered rational if viewed as a mechanism by which "citizens might punish their more favored (but still distant) party . . . [and force] it to move closer to them in future elections."[24]

Essentially the question one must ask about the twenties is: could nonvoting based on indifference or alienation or both reasonably be said to characterize particular segments of the population, thereby exacerbating the effects of immigration, enfranchisement, and generational change described above? Burnham would argue that the disjunction between the socioeconomic structure and the political system that emerged after 1896 exaggerated the normal "forgetting" process and therefore the level of nonparticipation. An interesting contemporary view does not speak to the idea of nonvoting per se but makes the point that to at least two socially and economically important groups in the population the policies of the Democratic and Republican parties might reasonably be equally repugnant. In a symposium titled "The Political Outlook in the U.S.," held at the University of Chicago in 1931, Paul Douglas said:

> And yet, despite all this [traditional loyalties to the parties], it seems—to me, at least—that the existing alignment of parties and of party policy is fundamentally inconsistent with those fundamental economic alignments which furnish the taproots from which both parties and political sentiment must ultimately spring. Very briefly, the thesis which I wish to defend is that both the Republican and Democratic parties are now primarily business parties, operating consciously or unconsciously through their policies and ideas to protect the interests of the owners of industrial and commercial capital, and that they do not represent the interests of the two most economically important classes in the country, namely, the urban and town wage-workers and the farmers.[25]

The first thirty years of the twentieth century saw three significant and related processes at work: immigration, urbanization, and industrialization. The rate of growth of large cities was at its peak in the early decades of the century. The proportion of the population living in places of 100,000 or more increased from 18.7 percent to 26 percent in the years between 1900 and 1920, while it increased by less than three percentage points, to 28.7 percent, from 1920 to 1940.[26] This impressive growth was augmented by the immigrants of 1890–1910, who in contrast to earlier arrivals were primarily urban dwellers. About this period Taeuber and Taeuber say:

> The majority of the immigrants . . . were Europeans who landed in the ports of entry with little education, skills or capital. The needs in the United States involved primarily unskilled or semiskilled labor. The initial distribution of immigrants was related to the accessible places where employment was available. Consequently, the major concentrations were in New England, the Middle Atlantic states and the industrial region around the Great Lakes.[27]

In 1920, the foreign-born population in states over 60 percent urban was 26 percent of the total; in contrast the foreign-born comprised only 2.8 percent of the population of states less than 15 percent urban. The same relationship holds for the level of industrialization: the less agricultural a state, the fewer foreign-born citizens it had. Or, looked at another way, in 1920 nearly 80 percent of the foreign-born whites lived in urban places, as compared with just 54 percent of native whites. Immigrants during this period listed their occupations mostly as household workers, craftsmen, and laborers.[28]

In 1896 it was these types of people—city dwellers, workers, immigrants—who provided McKinley's margin of victory. Aside from the particular issue of free silver, which at least temporarily united all classes of urbanites against Bryan and the Democrats, Degler argues that in a more general sense it was rational for urban immigrants to support the national Republican party well into the twentieth century.[29]

> The party and its leaders had not hesitated to use the national power in behalf of economic growth by sponsoring such measures as the Homestead Act, land grants and loans to railroad construction companies, and protective tariffs. . . . This nationalistic tradition and these specific measures . . . added up to a national image of the party that would appeal to urban voters and immigrants.[30]

Woodrow Wilson did damage the Republican hold on these groups. Binkley goes so far as to cite Wilson's labor legislation as a "neglected landmark" in the history of American political parties, since progressive labor laws had until then been largely Republican legislation.[31] During Wilson's second administration, however, Democratic support for the League of Nations and the Versailles Treaty alienated many immigrant groups. Nativist, rural, dry forces and anti-nativist, urban, wet forces collided all during the twenties in the Democratic party, and until 1928 the former coalition was more or less dominant, a fact which was reflected in the Democratic platforms. Though the Republicans had become markedly less sympathetic to labor with the passing of the McKinley-Roosevelt-Hanna era, the Democrats must have seemed little better. In 1920, "The Democratic platform was hardly more forward looking than the Republican, which . . . contained a call for the recognition of the Soviet government, American participation in the World Court, and acknowledgement of labor's right to bargain collectively."[32]

Thus in the two policy areas which touched most directly the interests of the urban foreign-stock workers, there was in the twenties little difference between the parties. The Palmer raids of the 1920s temporarily, at least, identified a Democratic administration with the most antiradical, antiimmigrant of viewpoints. Meanwhile, one of the first acts of the new Republican administration was the Emergency Quota Act of 1921, restricting the number of yearly immigrants from a particular country to 3 percent of that country's U.S. residents in 1910. This quota was later constricted even further by the Immigration Act of 1924. Though the Republicans were more overtly xenophobic in their public pronouncements ("No alien should become a citizen until he has become genuinely American," stated their platform in 1920), it is significant that when the Immigration Act came to a vote in Congress, there was little difference in the voting behavior of Democrats and Republicans.[33]

The interests of labor per se got short shrift in both parties' platforms during the 1920s. There was very little mention, in fact, of any social welfare legislation. An examination of the Democratic and Republican platforms for 1920, 1924, and 1928 shows that the problems of agriculture played a prominent role, but that with regard to labor both parties contented themselves with perfunctory endorsements of the Child Labor Act, the principle of collective bargaining, and investigation of "abuses" of the power of injunction. Though the Democrats in 1924 and 1928 mentioned briefly the notion that public works projects should be created during periods of unemployment, in general there were virtually no visible differences between the parties on labor and related issues.

Douglas argued that policies in the interest of both urban workers and farmers would include social legislation, tariff reduction, the increasing use of income and inheritance taxes, stricter regulation of utilities, and the consideration of economic planning, but he also explained why neither the Democratic nor the Republican party was or was likely to be sympathetic to such reforms. The latter "is, with rare exceptions, openly the party of the business interests . . . one finds it, in general, to be directed by a powerful fusion of high finance [and] corrupt machines." When progressives such as Norris have attempted to press for reform, he says, the Republican organization has supported the Democrats. The Democratic party, however, "is fundamentally composed of conservative Southern elements, now strongly tinged with industrialism, and the corrupt political machines of Boston, New York, and Chicago. The leaders in this party are, moreover, anxious to win the favor of big business," as evidenced "strikingly" in 1928 by their "national abandonment of their historic low-tariff policy" and by the "widely-advertised pledge of seven Democratic leaders that they could be depended upon not to hurt business."[34]

In summary, it is perhaps a useful oversimplification to say that large segments of the population—in particular of the burgeoning urban working class—faced with the choice (at the presidential level) between a party that seemed to be the party of the wealthy establishment, on the one hand, and a party that had not yet shaken off the mantle of Bryanism, on the other, instead withdrew temporarily from politics. Given the politics of the twenties, this would not have been an unreasonable response.

Four

The Mobilization of the Nonimmunized:
A Reconstruction

If there were good survey data available from the twenties and thirties, it would be possible to determine whether the groups we have identified as being outside the electoral system in the earlier decade really did constitute the foundation of Roosevelt's victories. The demise of the famous *Literary Digest* poll, considered reasonably accurate and reliable until its notable failure to predict the 1936 election results, illustrates the unfortunate lack of such data.[1] Nevertheless, we have several alternative ways of establishing the plausibility of our argument. The first is through the use of voting returns and other aggregate data. On a national, state, or even county level such an exercise can lend credibility to the mobilization scenario, but this is as much as it can do. Even when this type of analysis is performed at the level of wards or precincts, as in the case study of Chicago voting patterns (see chap. 6), caution must be used in making inferences about individual behavior. In many of the previous studies of realignment the ecological fallacy does not represent a major peril. Generalizations about the timing, magnitude, or geographical locus of partisan shifts, for example, do not depend on conclusions about the behavior of individual citizens. But a study that proposes to describe the dynamics of realignment at the individual level is faced with much more serious problems of inference if it is based an aggregate data.

The second alternative, which is a possible solution to the ecological problem in this case though not in the study of preceding realignments, is the use of what might be called "retrospective" survey data. Questions asked in recent surveys, if they inquire about the respondents' past political behavior, may help to assess the relative validity of the mobilization and conversion models of the New Deal realignment. Use of these data brings its own problems, of course: people's memories can be unreliable to begin with, and aggregating many unreliable memories to draw conclusions about political behavior in the past is a risky enterprise.

Thus both the aggregate data analysis and the "retrospective" survey data analysis are problematic: neither should be seen as entirely convincing, but together they act in a mutually reinforcing way to establish the significance of the mobilization of nonimmunized groups. In particular, the aggregate analysis can be most useful in locating, geographically and ethnically, the sources of the increase in Democratic support, while the survey analysis can contribute to our knowledge of the role that new political generations played in the realignment.

Reconstructing Party Identification

How is it possible to use modern survey data —specifically the Survey Research Center election studies—as part of an analysis of the New Deal realignment? The 1952 survey, the earliest in the series, was conducted a full sixteen years after the New Deal realignment had been completed, and twenty to thirty years after the crucial prerealignment period of the 1920s. Nonetheless the surveys contain some relevant data. In eight election studies between 1952 and 1972, almost 15,000 citizens were interviewed.[2] Many of these people lived through the era under analysis. Among the 15,000 respondents must be some who switched from the Republican to the Democratic party in 1932 or 1936; and there must be many representatives of the young of the late 1920s who played such an important role in forming the new Democratic majority. Indeed, according to their age, about 1,800 were eligible to vote in 1920, and an additional 3,000 had entered the electorate by 1936.

Respondents in these surveys were asked their current party identification (i.e., whether they thought of themselves as Democrats, Republicans, or independents); they were also asked whether this identification had changed and, if so, when. In short, the 1952–72 surveys include the right people and the right questions; it is simply a matter of using this information in a way that will permit the description of aggregate changes in partisanship during the twenties and thirties. To this end the eight surveys can be combined so that all respondents are analyzed together as one data set, ignoring the fact that they were interviewed in different years.

The data on past and present party identification, combined with the year of birth, enable one to estimate the party preference of an individual in any year since that individual became a citizen. For example, a fifty-year-old respondent interviewed in 1958 says that she is currently a Republican but used to be a Democrat and reports having made that change in 1934. She would be categorized as a Democrat if the year we were interested in was 1930, but a Republican if we wanted her party identification in 1938. Most people, about 80 percent of our pooled samples, report never having changed party identification and can be assigned their current party identification at all points in time.[3]

In this way the party identifications of all respondents who were over twenty in a particular year can be calculated. Merely aggregating the past party preferences of all such citizens, however, will not provide an accurate historical estimate of the partisan division, because the age distribution of the population shifts over time. An age cohort that constituted 15 percent of the adult population in 1936 might, twenty years later, when a sample is drawn for a survey, constitute only 10 percent. It is necessary to know the distribution of age groups in the population in the year for which we want to describe the country's partisan makeup. Then the age cohorts in the pooled sample can be weighted by the proportion they were of the population in that earlier year.

Table 4 is an example of the method by which the party identification of the population can be "reconstructed" for any given year. In this example, the proportion Democratic for the year 1940 is calculated. The respondents who were in the electorate at that time are first divided into eleven age groups; the period of birth is given in column a, their ages in 1940 in column b. Column c reports the proportion of the population each of these age groups was, according to the 1940 census.[4] Each respondent is assigned a party identification for 1940. This is done as described above, by assigning a respondent his current party identification if he reports never changing and by assign-

Table 4   Sample Reconstruction of Party Identification: Percentage Democratic of the 1940 Population

Age Group		Proportion of Population in Each Age Group, 1940 (c)	Percentage Democratic in Each Age Group in 1940 (d)	Contribution of Each Group to Percent Democratic (c × d) (e)
Period of Birth (a)	Ages in 1940 (b)			
1916–19	21–24	.109	.581	.075
1911–15	25–29	.131	.588	.077
1906–10	30–34	.133	.536	.071
1901–5	35–39	.113	.543	.061
1896–1900	40–44	.104	.507	.053
1891–95	45–49	.097	.478	.046
1886–90	50–54	.085	.491	.042
1881–85	55–59	.068	.503	.034
1876–80	60–65	.056	.495	.028
pre-1876	over 65	.106	.445	.047

$\Sigma = 52.2\% =$ Reconstructed Percent Democratic in 1940

Source   Reports of current party identifications are from the Survey Research Center/Center for Political Studies Election Studies of 1952, 1956, 1958, 1960, 1964, 1968, 1970, and 1972.

ing "changers" to the party that their date of change tells us they supported in 1940. The resultant percentage of Democrats in each age group is reported in column d. To take into account both the extent to which the group identified with the Democrats and the group's relative size in 1940, the proportion Democratic (column d) is multiplied by the group's size (c). The result, in column e, is the group's contribution to the total amount of Democratic support.

For example, the group that was 30–34 in 1940 was 13.3 percent of the adult population in 1940. According to the retrospective questions, 53.6 percent of the group were Democrats in 1940. The product of these percentages is the contribution to the Democrats of this age cohort. Summing the entries in in column e for all the age cohorts gives the reconstructed proportion of those identifying as Democrats in the population in 1940, 52.2 percent.

Some Tests of the Validity
of the Reconstruction

There are a number of reasons why such retrospective reconstruction might engender a certain unease. For one thing, people's memories may be inaccurate. This would be particularly devastating for our estimates if there were systematic distortion—for instance, more remember early support for the Democrats than was actually the case because that party is currently the more popular of the two. Another weakness of the method has to do with death rates. This particular weighting procedure deals with overall mortality rates, but it does not deal with the possibility that the supporters of one party may live longer than supporters of the other, thereby resulting in later years in a biased sample. If Republicans live longer than Democrats, for example, Republicans would at present be overrepresented in the age cohorts that participated in the politics of the twenties and thirties.[5]

There are several ways, however, of checking the accuracy of our estimates. First, the Survey Research Center data themselves can be used as a standard against which to measure the reconstructed party identifications. Data gathered in 1968,

1970, and 1972 can be used to calculate the citizenry's partisan preferences in 1952 and 1956. The 1952 and 1956 surveys then give us a measure against which to check our estimates. Table 5 compares the reconstruction of partisanship in these two years on the basis of the 1968–72 surveys with the responses actually obtained in 1952 and 1956. As can be seen from this table, the estimates are very similar to the actual distributions of party identification in the earlier years. The

Table 5   Reconstruction of 1952 and 1956 Party Identification, Compared with SRC Party Identification

	Demo-cratic	Inde-pendent	Repub-lican
1952			
Reconstruction	51%	18%	31%
SRC 1952 Study	49	23	28
1956			
Reconstruction	51	20	29
SRC 1956 Study	45	24	30

differences between the reconstruction and the earlier data, in fact, are no larger than the differences between the SRC and Gallup Poll results for party identification in those years (from surveys conducted within three months of one another).[6] The slight underestimation of independents is to be expected, since the one partisan shift that cannot be measured adequately is from independent to Democrat or Republican. Thus, for example, a few individuals who may have been independent in 1952 or 1956 but were moved to identify with the Democrats during the Kennedy era would be counted as having always been Democrats. The slight discrepancy between the reconstruction and the contemporary data shows a smaller Democratic advantage, especially in 1956—which is also explainable. Party identification if asked close to election time may reflect the vote intentions of some respondents rather than their underlying party loyalty, and 1952 and 1956 were, of course, Republican presidential victories.

Comparisons between the reconstruction and some earlier data are also possible. The earliest questions on party identification were asked in 1937 by the Gallup organization. Table 6 compares the reconstruction for 1937 with the party identification data from the Gallup study of that year. The figures are similar; the reconstruction concurs almost completely with the proportion Democratic, Republican, and independent reported by Gallup in 1937.

Table 6   Reconstruction of 1937 Party Identification Compared with Gallup 1937 Party Identification

	Democratic	Independent	Republican
Reconstruction	53%	12%	34%
Gallup 1937	53	16	32

Finally, one can deal more directly with the possibilities of systematic memory distortion and unequal mortality rates between the two parties. This can be done by reconstructing the 1937 party identification twice: once from the surveys conducted in 1952, 1956, and 1958, and once with the surveys conducted in 1968, 1970, and 1972. If either systematic bias exists—biased memory or differential death rates—the reconstruction based on the earlier surveys should be more accurate. Table 7 presents the Gallup 1937 data on party identification, a reconstruction of the 1937 electorate based on the surveys conducted in 1952, 1956, and 1958, and a reconstruction based

Table 7   Reconstruction of 1937 Party Identification Based on 1952, 1956, 1958 Data and 1968, 1970, 1972 Data, Compared with Gallup 1937 Party Identification

	Democratic	Independent	Republican
Reconstruction (1952–58 data)	53%	12%	35%
Reconstruction (1968–72 data)	54	14	32
Gallup 1937	53	16	32

on the 1968, 1970, and 1972 surveys. The differences between
the two reconstructions are minimal. If there is any tendency
for Republicans to outlive Democrats, using a group of relatively elderly people (as is done with the 1968, 1970, 1972
data) to reconstruct party identification at an earlier time would
produce a distortion in a Republican direction. The fact that
the estimate of 1937 party identification using the 1952, 1956,
1958 data is in fact more Republican than the estimate using
the 1968, 1970, 1972 data indicates that this kind of distortion is not taking place. The same logic leads to a rejection of
the hypothesis of systematic bias in memory, since any such
bias would be more apparent in the later surveys.

Changes in Party
Identification, 1920–74

The "memory" data appear accurate, and
therefore the reconstruction of past party identification can
proceed with somewhat more confidence. Figure 10 presents
the reconstructed party identification of Americans from 1920
through 1948 and the party identification reported by respondents in the SRC election studies from 1952 through 1974. It
documents clearly the dramatic changes in the party system
during the past sixty years. In contrast to the strong two-party
system of 1920, the United States party system now has as
many independents as Democrats, while the Republicans claim
the loyalty of less than 20 percent of the population. The
change can be divided into several periods.

Period 1: Realignment, 1920–36. In 1920 each party, according to this reconstruction, claimed about the same number
of followers and less than 10 percent of the population was independent. Over the next sixteen years the proportion of independents remained basically stable, while the Democrats gained
ground steadily at the expense of the Republicans. By 1936,
the reconstruction estimates the population to have become 53
percent Democratic, 36 percent Republican and 12 percent independent: a thirteen percentage point redistribution in the
strength of the two major parties.

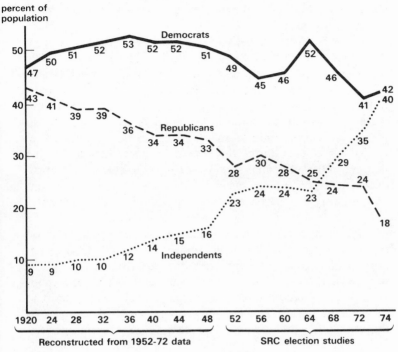

Figure 10   Party identification, 1920–74

Period 2: Stabilization, 1936–52. In the next period Democratic support declined slightly. The proportion of Republicans
also continued to decline, though not as precipitously as in the
preceding period. In fact, the Republican share of the electorate
remained fairly stable from 1936 to 1948, which accords with
Sundquist's description of the "aftershocks" of the New Deal
realignment, during which Republicans as well as Democrats
made gains in some areas.[7] Perhaps the most interesting point
to be made about this era is that once the realignment had been
accomplished, the number of independents began to grow, rising from 12 percent in 1936 to 23 percent in 1952. It is as if
the highly potent political issues that produce the realignment
polarize the population into two partisan camps but, having
done so, gradually lose their salience. The partisan pull is less

strong, and once again the number of people who are loyal to neither party grows.

Period 3: No net change, 1952–64. The survey data from the 1950s and early 1960s show a decline of the Democrats in the Eisenhower era and a resurgence at the time of the Kennedy administration. A further slight decrease occurs in the proportion of the population who identify with the Republicans, but there is no major alteration in the relative strength of the two parties. The proportion of independents in the population remains stable. It is during this essentially static period that the first and most influential survey-based voting studies were produced. It is perhaps not surprising that one of their major conclusions was that party attachment is a lifelong commitment.

Period 4: Decline of the parties, 1964–74. Since 1964 the partisan composition of the population has undergone the most rapid change of the sixty years under consideration. The proportion of Democratic supporters dropped from a high of 52 percent in 1964 to 42 percent ten years later, while the Republican party suffered a three percentage point drop in support in the same period. Meanwhile, the proportion of independents in the population grew from 25 percent to 38 percent between 1964 and 1974.

The Role of New Generations in the Realignment

Butler and Stokes, two of the many observers who have commented on the significance of "political generations," point out that the distribution of party support in Britain in the mid 1960s "can be accounted for in terms of the impress of early political forces on the young and the preservation of these forces in the hardening allegiances of later years." "We must ask not how old the elector is," they continue, "but when it was that he was young."[8]

In the preceding chapter it was argued that being young in the twenties may well have predisposed one to political apathy and partisan disaffection. Many of those people coming of age in this period were what Beck calls the "children of normalcy," and many more, as children of immigrants, can be seen as outside his three-generation model of the socialization process altogether. One might expect, then, that as far as they are able, our data will show that the young played a significant role in the 1928–36 period of partisan change.

To examine the party preferences of the various age cohorts at the time they began to vote, the retrospective questions can be used to calculate the party identification distribution of a particular four-year age cohort when that cohort was 21 to 24 years old. Since our concern is with only one age cohort at a time, no weights need be involved. Figure 11 displays the party preferences of entering cohorts—based on contemporary surveys from 1952 onward and on the respondents' recollections for the earlier years. The data show, for example, that the age

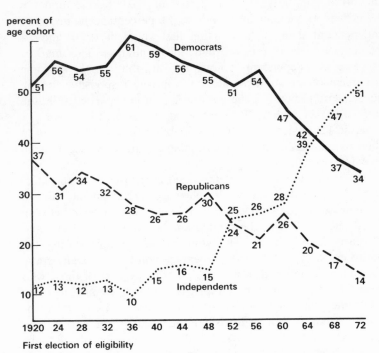

Figure 11   Party identification of age cohorts at entrance into the electorate (those entering between 1920 and 1948 based on reconstructed data)

cohort first able to vote in 1948 was 51 percent Democratic, 30 percent Republican, and 15 percent independent. This figure demonstrates the responsiveness of the young to the political temper of the times. The degree to which the entering cohort identified with the Republican party was highest in 1920; the Democratic share of the entering cohort was at its peak with the group that first voted in 1936. Close examination of the trends in figure 11 indicates the impact that new voters may have on the shape of the electorate. For example, the decreasing frequency with which the Democrats during the last two Roosevelt administrations recruited new young voters and the concomitant resurgence of the Republican party among the same group contributed to the decline in Democratic support from 1948 to 1956 and the stability of Republican support in the fifties. Similarly, the group that entered the electorate in 1964 was 39 percent independent, 11 percentage points more independent than the group that first voted in 1960, and 14 percentage points more so than the population. This marked increase in independents among a group that was at the time 9 percent of the adult population is largely responsible for the subsequent growth in the proportion of independents in the population as a whole. In addition, it is obvious from figure 11 that the Republicans' continuing inability to win new voters to their side has had cumulative, damaging effects on Republican strength over the years.[9]

To look more closely at the cohorts who entered the electorate around the time of the New Deal realignment, table 8 compares the youngest citizens in each election year between 1920 and 1940 with the population as we have reconstructed its party identification. The youngest age groups during the entire era were around five percentage points more Democratic than the population as a whole. Sixty-one percent of those who were 21–24 in 1936, for example, recall being Democrats then, while the population at that time was only 53 percent Democratic. What is more surprising, the groups that entered the electorate in 1920, 1924, and 1928 (a time when the Republican party should have been most successful in recruiting young citizens) were also substantially more Democratic than the population. Once again, it is essential to note that many of the "Democrats" we obtain with the recall data were not really Democrats in the 1920s. They were Democrats when they were interviewed, in 1952 or 1964 or 1972, and said in addition that they had "never changed" their party identification. But it is possible, indeed almost certain, that most of these citizens fell into the "nonimmunized," apolitical group in the twenties.

Table 8   Percent Democratic (Reconstructed) of 21–24 Year Olds and Population, 1920–40

Election Year	Percent Democratic	
	21–24	Population
1920	51	47
1924	56	50
1928	54	51
1932	55	52
1936	61	53
1940	59	52

If the young citizens during the twenties and thirties had entered the electorate with the same partisan makeup as the rest of the citizenry, substantial conversion of Republicans would have been necessary to effect the redistribution of party support that occurred between 1920 and 1936. Instead, each successive group that came of age in the twenties was different (more Democratic, less Republican) from the populace it joined. This apparent Democratic bias in the partisanship of the young had the cumulative effect of changing the partisan balance from a relatively even division to a clear Democratic majority. In fact, one can easily (if crudely) estimate the amount of partisan redistribution that was accounted for by the partisan bias of the young rather than by conversion. By starting with the partisan split we estimate for 1920, applying the appropriate mortality rates to both Democrats and non-Democrats, and adding to the population entering cohorts who are proportionately Democratic and non-Democratic (see fig. 11), one can produce over 60 percent of the increase in Democratic identification which occurred according to the reconstruction. This is a conservative estimate, however, of the role of the young, since the mortality rates for Republicans, a generally older group, are bound to have been higher than for Democrats. The voting behavior of the young during the realignment era also supports the notion of a youthful surge toward the Democrats as a factor contributing to the realignment. Table 9 shows that, of those who cast their first presidential vote in 1924 and were 28 or under at the time, 80 percent voted for Roosevelt.[10] In 1936, while FDR received 62 percent of the two-party vote nationally, the first voters under 28 gave him an extraordinary majority of 85 percent.

Table 9   Recalled First Vote of Voters 28 or Under, 1920–40, Compared with National Vote

	Percent Democratic	
Election Year	Among first voters	Of national two-party vote
1920	30	35
1924	28	35
1928	47	41
1932	80	59
1936	85	62
1940	66	55

Source   Survey Research Center 1952 Election Study.

The data in table 9 pose a puzzle, however. In contrast to the voters coming of age during the New Deal period, young voters who came of age in the early twenties remember giving proportionately fewer votes to the Democratic presidential candidates than did the population as a whole. This seems inconsistent with the high proportion of acknowledged Democrats found among those who were young in the 1920s (in table 8). A similar discrepancy occurs when the general population is considered. Our party identification reconstruction (fig. 10) shows a Democratic majority as early as 1920, yet the Democrats did not win a majority of the presidential or congressional vote until 1932. These apparent contradictions will be resolved in the next section.

Realignment as the Mobilization
of "Potential" Democrats

There is a gap in the data on which the reconstruction of party identification is based. Democrats are questioned about whether they ever considered themselves Republicans, and vice versa; independents are asked if they were ever Republicans or Democrats. Those who presently identify with a party are not, however, asked whether they used to be independent. Nor are party identifiers asked (and perhaps this would be an impossible question) when they began to regard themselves as Democrats or Republicans. The fact that a Democrat says he has "never changed" his party identification (80 percent of all party identifiers fall into this category) can mean many things. It can mean that his parents were Democrats, that he always considered himself a Democrat and that he began voting for Democrats as soon as he was legally able to do so. It could mean, however, that he has never identified with the Republican party, but did not come to think of himself as a Democrat until age 30 or 40. If this person had been queried about his party affiliation at age 25, he would probably have said "independent" or "no party" rather than "Democrat." This does not alter the important fact that this person was never a Republican. He may have identified with the Democrats ever since he came of age, or he may have been moved to support the Democrats after having been independent or apolitical for many years. But he is not a Republican convert.

In a political system with high participation or one with compulsory voting, this gap in the information we have about individuals' partisanship would be less important. Virtually everyone could be said to have acquired a party identification quite early in their careers as citizens. This is not the case in the United States, where 40 percent or more of the electorate fails to vote in presidential elections, where in 1952, 35 percent of the SRC's sample declared that they had *never* voted in a presidential election. People acquire and, more importantly, translate into behavior their party identifications at many different points in their lives.

Suppose we assume that a person who reports "never switching" party identification acquired that identification, not when she came of voting age, but when she cast her first vote. This would change our estimate of party identification in the 1920s substantially since, in general, the majority of people who came of age in the 1920s did not vote until much later. Of those who entered the electorate between 1920 and 1928, 39 percent do not report having voted until at least the third election in which they were eligible.

The question asked in 1952 on respondents' first vote can be used to calculate the proportion of each entering cohort between 1920 and 1940 who voted in the first election in which they were eligible. Figure 12 presents these data for respondents who in 1952 categorized themselves as Republicans or Democrats who had "never switched." This figure shows clearly that the "never switched" Democrats comprised the majority of the youthful nonvoters in the 1920s. Of the people who came into the electorate between 1924 and 1928, for example, 29 percent

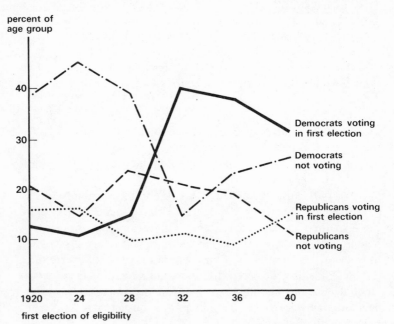

Figure 12   Voting behavior of Democrats and Republicans at age of entry into the electorate, 1920–40

were "never switched" Democrats who did not vote in the 1924 election, while only 10 percent were "never switched" Republicans who did not vote. The young Republicans who voted in 1924 outnumbered their Democratic contemporaries. The higher Republican participation holds true for the entire decade; it explains the discrepancy between the large proportion of Democrats we seem to find among the young of the 1920s and the predominantly Republican voting behavior of the "first voters" of that era.

After 1932 the voting behavior of those who would later call themselves Democrats changed dramatically. The majority of young Democrats who entered the electorate voted as soon as they were able. Over 70 percent of those who were 21–24 and who were "never switched" Democrats voted in 1932. In both 1932 and 1936, there were twice as many voting Democrats as voting Republicans among the youngest citizens.

Let us return to our assumption that an individual who reports she has always supported a party and has never switched adopted that partisan identification not when she entered the electorate but at the time of her first vote. The data just presented would mean that a large number of people came of political age in the 1920s, but did not take on a party identification because they did not vote. When they were mobilized to vote in 1928 or 1932 or 1936, most voted Democratic and also took on a Democratic identification which they never dropped. (This is why they appear in the later surveys as people who have always been Democrats.) In addition, another large group of voters come of age between 1928 and 1936. They voted as soon as they were legally able and most of these people also became Democrats. The surge in the Democratic vote in 1932 and 1936 came primarily from these two newly mobilized groups.

Party Identification and Voting:
Another Look at the Reconstruction

Estimates of past party identification can be revised, in the light of this argument, by using responses to the 1952 question on first vote. In 1928, for example, it has been estimated that the population was 51 percent Democratic, 39 percent Republican, and 10 percent independent. But many of these people had never voted in a presidential election. The 1952 survey contains information on when Democrats and Republicans of a particular age began to vote. In 1928, for instance, 28 percent of the Democrats just eligible to vote did so. And only 40 percent of the Democrats aged 40–44 in 1928 had voted in a presidential election in that year or previously. Thus one can arrive at an estimate of the proportion of nonvoting and voting Democrats (and Republicans) in each of the age groups we used to reconstruct party identification for 1928. The same method of weighting each age group according to its share of the 1928 population is followed to derive an estimate of the proportion of voting and nonvoting Democrats or Republicans in that year. In this case, the estimation is that 39 percent of the 1928 Democrats had voted in a presidential election at some time but 61 percent had not done so. They can be labelled "potential" Democrats, since we know they will eventually think of themselves as Democrats. But in 1928 it is likely that they were apolitical. In the same way, we calculate that 66 percent of the 1928 Republicans had voted, while 34 percent were "potential" Republicans. Thus the 1928 population is broken down in the following manner: 20 percent Democrats; 26 percent Republicans; 32 percent "potential" Democrats; 13 percent "potential" Republicans; 10 percent independents. In figure 13 we present a reconstruction of the electorate into these categories over the years between 1920 and 1940. The data account quite well for the changes that took place in the party alignment during that period. At the beginning of the period, a mere 14 percent of the population consisted of Democrats who had voted in presidential elections. Thirty-four percent were "potential" Democrats who did not vote. The number of potential Republicans was also greater in 1920 than the number of voting Republicans. In all we estimate that in 1920, 34 percent of the citizens were voters, 57 percent were nonvoters, and 9 percent were independent. This agrees roughly with Burnham's characterization of the twenties as a decade in which "hardly more than one-third of the eligible adults were . . . core voters.

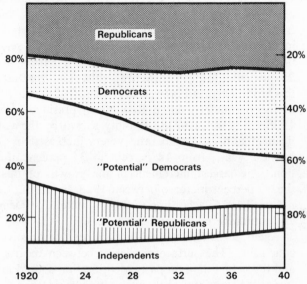

Figure 13   Party identification and voting, 1920–40 (adult population reconstructed from pooled SRC/CPS studies) The term "potential" refers here to those people who were not voting in the particular election but who were *later* to become actively identifying Republicans or Democrats.

Another one-sixth were peripheral voters and fully one-half remained outside the active voting universe altogether."[11]

By 1940, in contrast, the Democrats' position had completely reversed itself; 34 percent of the population was classed as voting Democrats and only 14 percent as potential Democrats. Nonvoting among Republicans had decreased at about the same rate as nonvoting among Democrats. However, since the number of Republicans in the population had decreased (from 43 percent to 34 percent), the proportion of voting Republicans increased only six percentage points between 1920 and 1940, compared with the 20 percent growth among Democrats.

In summary, the reconstruction suggests that the changes in party identification and voting behavior that took place between

1920 and 1940 were the following. The proportion of independents remained stable during the twenties, but increased from 10 percent to 14 percent between 1932 and 1940. Voting Republicans were also a relatively stable segment of the population, varying between 20 and 27 percent and averaging 24 percent during the twenty years. The greatest increase in this group occurred between 1924 and 1928, which corresponds to the particularly large Republican presidential vote cast in 1928. In contrast to the stability shown by the voting Republican identifiers, Democratic voters increased by 150 percent in these years, from 14 percent to 34 percent of the population. The largest increment in the growth of this group was the 30 percent increase between 1928 and 1932, though it was not until 1936, according to this estimate, that Democratic voters outnumbered Republican voters.[12]

Again, these data should be considered suggestive rather than conclusive. The surface similarity between the reconstructions and the actual data on party identification should not lead us to forget the very real problems that always attend the use of recall data and are especially serious when respondents are asked to cast their memories back over many years. The safest conclusion to be drawn is that these rather precarious data appear in a general way to be consonant with the argument being advanced, but that firmer empirical support for the argument can best be provided by imaginative use of aggregate data, both in the present work and, in the future, by other scholars.

Five

The Conservation of Partisanship

Partisan loyalty has often been presented as an enduring individual attribute, but one quite likely to undergo substantial change during periods of political crisis (see chap. 1). If in fact the great political upheaval around the time of the New Deal (seen in terms of partisanship, that is) occurred mainly through mobilization of the nonimmunized and replacement of the electorate rather than through conversion, the status of party identification as a "secular religion" is greatly enhanced. In this view, even during the traumas of the Depression and the emergence of new bases of cleavage between the parties, individuals' partisan attachments remained relatively stable.

Assigning as it does the weight of the change to new members of the electorate, many of whom are just entering adulthood, this perspective can be (and has been) seen as presenting problems for yet another component of the "Michigan model" of party identification. In a nutshell: partisanship is said to be largely an inherited characteristic (as would be expected of a secular religion). The parents of the "New Deal generation" could be expected to be predominantly Republican in partisan coloration, since the majority of their political experience would have occurred during the "system of 1896" period of Republican domination. Thus one is faced with the question of where, exactly, all these enthusiastic new Democrats came from. It has been repeatedly shown that children of partisan parents who opt for identification with the other party (as opposed to those who come to consider themselves independents) are very rare. A reexamination of some of the data presented in *The American Voter* (chap. 7) indicates that the number of citizens who identify with the party opposite that of their parents is very small: only 12 percent of those whose parents were in agreement on party preference considered themselves (in 1958) to be supporters of the other party.[1]

Nonetheless, if we are to explain the realignment without much recourse to Republican-Democratic conversion, it seems as if times of political crisis or change must act to weaken the normal intergenerational transmission of partisanship: those Democrats must have come from Republican families. This is the assumption at the basis of some recent work by Philip Converse and Paul Beck, each of whom has advanced an explanation for this puzzle.[2] Here I will try to show, briefly, why neither of these explanations is necessary and to suggest that the "inheritance" component of the model, like the "stability" component, need not be completely discarded in explaining this particular realignment phase.

Was There a "Loosening" of Partisan Ties?

Beck presents a plausible if rather speculative (vis-à-vis the New Deal period, at least) argument about the impact of the political environment on the process of partisan socialization. The notion that strength and stability of partisanship vary according to one's parents' and one's own formative political experiences is reasonable, and undoubtedly the aggregate disengagement of the young (as well as other citizens) was a necessary condition for the realignment. But Beck's statement that "a majority of these first [Roosevelt] voters came from Republican homes" is erroneous—and his subsequent explanation of the phenomenon less than convincing—because of his implicit assumption that *all* families in the U.S. just before the realignment were "partisan," whether Democratic or Republican. This ignores the recent wave of immigrants (nearly a third of the relevant age group had at least one foreign-born parent) and the unusually low level of voter mobilization (and hence, in all probability, of partisanship) during the 1920s.

An initial examination of the relevant data offers little evidence for an across-the-board decline in the intergenerational continuity of partisanship. Of SRC election study respondents born between 1908 and 1915, and therefore able to cast their first votes in the elections of 1932 and 1936, 59 percent place themselves in the same general partisan camp as their parents. If one ignores for the moment problems with misperception and/or recall, it is interesting to note that this figure is identical to the proportion of 1965 high school seniors, in Jennings and Niemi's 1968 study, whose partisanship matched that of their parents.[3] This provides at least minimal evidence that there was not, in the 1930s, a wholesale rejection of parental partisan cues.

The Possibility of Misperception

Converse wants to retain the notions of "generalized party convictions of individuals" and of the "high continuity of the parent-child partisanship bond," and still understand how the realignment could have taken place. To do this, he posits massive misperception. That is, children saw their nominally Republican parents voting for FDR in 1932 and perhaps 1936; the children "took them to be Democrats" (even though the parents may have returned to their party later) and thereafter could "consider themselves as Democrats without any particular sense of disjuncture with the partisanship of their parents, at least as they perceived that partisanship."[4]

The most glaring error in this explanation is one simply of chronology. The parental cohorts who, according to the recall of their children, are being misperceived as Democrats were born in 1895–1905. (That many of these people were undoubtedly the children of immigrants and may not have acquired any party identification at all until after 1928 is unfortunately over-looked.) Assuming an average thirty-year age difference be-tween generations, the children with whom Converse proposes to explain the realignment were born between 1925 and 1935! Even if one assumes only a twenty-five year difference, they would have been born between 1920 and 1930—certainly old enough, as Converse says, to be influenced by their parents' al-leged defection to Roosevelt in the thirties, but certainly *not* themselves old enough to contribute to the "sharply Democratic coloration of [the] cohorts entering the electorate during the 1930s." Thus, misperception as Converse describes it may well account, for example, for the particularly high rate of Demo-cratic identification ascribed to parents by children who entered the electorate in the early 1940s, but it does not help us ac-count for the new Democrats who helped create the Roosevelt majorities of 1932 and 1936.

The Possibility of Distortion

It is true that the "children of the New Deal" remember their parents as being more heavily Democratic than we might expect them to be. Table 10 shows how fathers of people who entered the electorate in the early thirties are de-scribed by their children. Of those recalled as having a definite partisanship, 62 percent are remembered as being Democrats when their children were growing up. The idea that over 45 percent of this parental generation identified with the Demo-

Table 10	Recall of Father's Partisanship by "New Deal" Generation (born 1908–15)	
	Father is recalled as:	
	Democrat	46.9%
	Republican	28.6
	No partisan cue	24.6
	a) don't know	9.6
	b) independent	4.3
	c) apolitical, not citizen, etc.	10.7

Source   Pooled SRC/CPS Election Studies (see table 1).

crats and less than 30 percent with the Republicans is counter-intuitive, to be sure. Assuming, again, a thirty-year age differ-ence between generations, the parents in question were born between 1878 and 1885. Their first votes would have been cast during the Republican years at the turn of the century. How-ever, two factors do offer themselves as possible explanations of this apparently substantial distortion.

To begin with, the respondents' parents cannot, of course, be considered a representative sample of the population at some earlier point in time. And in this particular case, their nonrep-resentativeness would act to produce precisely the type of "dis-tortion" apparent in the SRC recall data. The fertility rates for women of the social groups that would later form the basis of the new Democratic coalition were a good deal higher than those of women in traditionally Republican groups. For ex-ample, in 1910 the birth rate for native 20–24 year-old women was 610 children per 1000 women; for foreign-born women in the same age group the birth rate was 712. Similar differences existed among women in their thirties and forties.[5] Lubell, in a section entitled "A Little Matter of Birth Rates," imbues these figures with vivid reality:

> Searching for families of five or more, the U.S. Immigration Commission's investigators [in 1910] found two-and-a-half times as many among unskilled laborers as among business-men. In Minneapolis, for example, the second generation of English stock—the backbone of Republican strength—celebrated a blessed event on the average of once every five years. Among the foreign born a new baby arrived every three years. As late as 1925 wives of miners and laborers were still having twice as many children as the wives of bankers.[6]

Such discrepancies among social groups in the rate at which they produced children could, obviously, account for much of the apparent overestimation of Democratic parents that we have found. Let us suppose that people in (roughly) their child-bearing years in 1910 were 50 percent Republican, 40 percent Democratic, and 10 percent independent. If the Democrats and independents each produced, on the average, 1.5 children to the Republicans' one each, the next generation, if all passed on their partisanship successfully, would be composed of 40 percent Republicans, 48 percent Democrats, and 12 percent independents. This figuring is purely speculative, of course, but it illustrates how differential birth rates could produce the illusion of massive misperception or defective memory on the part of the younger generation.

Second, many of those in the parental generation, particularly those (fairly large in number) who were immigrants, could undoubtedly be termed "potential" Democrats (see chap. 4). In other words, they were the nonvoters, the apoliticals, the independents of the 1920s and perhaps the "delayed first voters" of the 1930s who gave Roosevelt such resounding majorities.[7] Their children, asked twenty or thirty years later, may well remember either their parents' post-Depression Democratic support or, in fact, their prerealignment inactive Democratic tendencies. If one assumes that turnout among Republicans was much greater than turnout among Democrats before 1928, then basing an estimate of the distribution of partisan loyalties on the vote (which we have, in effect, done) produces an overestimation of the number of Republican identifiers.

Taking the birth rate argument and the "inactive Democrat" argument together, it begins to seem as if the "distortion" may be more apparent than real. In the next sections the recall data will be used—again in an illustrative manner—to attempt to identify the sources of Democratic gains among new voters in the thirties.

Conservation of Partisanship

With the SRC questions on past party identification and on parental partisanship, we can focus on the period of potential generational cleavage (the early 1930s) and examine the relationship between the partisan preferences of new voters at that time and the partisan preferences of their parents.[8]

Table 11 relates the party identification of cohorts entering the electorate between 1929 and 1936 to the (recalled) partisanship of their fathers. (For calculation of the former measure, see chap. 4.) Fathers' partisanship has been coded into three categories: Democrat, Republican, and those giving their chil-

Table 11   Earliest Partisanship of "New Deal" Generation by
Father's Partisanship*

		Party identification at entry into electorate (1929–36)			
		Dem.	Rep.	Ind.	
	Dem.	37.2	5.9	4.3	47.4
Recalled partisanship of father	Rep.	8.4	16.7	3.6	28.7
	no partisan cues†	13.0	5.2	5.6	23.8
					N = 2490

*The format of tables 11 and 13 is based on tables
11.6 and 11.7 in Butler and Stokes, *Political Change*.
Figures for parental party differ slightly from those
in table 10 because those respondents with missing
data on the party identification variable were excluded from this table.
   †The category includes those whose children recalled no party preference for them, independents,
"apoliticals," supporters of minor parties, and non-
citizens who supported neither party.

dren no Democratic or Republican cues. The latter group
includes those whose father's partisanship was not known or
recalled, independents, "apoliticals," and those who were said
to be nonpartisan because they were not citizens; it also includes those respondents who had no father or father surrogate. This is obviously a very diverse category, including, for
example, people who may have transmitted a strong preference
for the Socialist party to their children as well as people who
were completely apolitical. What justifies their combination is
that in none of these instances did the child grow up in an
explicitly Democratic or Republican milieu.

   Table 11 suggests that in the aggregate, the Republicans
did not lose strength from generation to generation: 28.7
percent of the parents were recalled as being Republicans, and

27.8 percent of the respondents were Republicans at the time of their entry into the electorate. The big change is in the percentage of each generation that is independent (or variously nonpartisan, in the case of the father). While almost a quarter of the parental generation can be so identified, only 13.5 percent of the children were independents in the 1930s.

Another consideration of possible bias in recall should be introduced at this point. Richard Niemi's study of high school seniors and their parents in 1965 indicates a bias in the students' accounts of their parents' partisanship which echoed the political tone of the time.[9] In other words, children stated that their parents had voted for Johnson when they had actually voted for Goldwater, and to some extent they stated that their parents were Democrats when they were actually Republicans. Since bias could plausibly be operating in the same direction in the present case, Niemi's figures on the amount of bias in student perceptions of parents' partisanship can be used to approximate the resultant distortion. The recalculation of Niemi's figures in table 12, for example, indicates that 77.6 percent of

Table 12   Perceptions of Parent's Party by High School Students, 1965

| | Students say their parents are: | | |
Parents are:	Democrats	Independents	Republicans
Democrats	77.6%	33.8%	11.8%
Independents	16.4	50.3	15.7
Republicans	6.0	15.9	72.4
	100.0	100.0	99.9
	N = 854	N = 320	N = 490

Source   Figures in this table are recalculated from the data in Table 3.3 in Richard G. Niemi, *How Family Members Perceive Each Other* (New Haven: Yale University Press, 1974), p. 59.

the students who identified their parent as a Democrat were correct; 16.4 percent of those parents so identified were actually independent, and 6 percent were Republicans.[10] If these percentages are applied as a corrective to the figures presented in table 11, we find that the distribution of partisanship in the parental generation is altered only slightly. The corrected distribution, allowing for the type of bias Niemi found, is 48.3 percent Democrat, 27.4 percent Republican, and 24.3 percent independent—certainly not significantly different from the distribution of parental party preferences as recalled by the respondents. Of course the bias introduced by faulty memory after the lapse of a fairly long period of time may be greater than that resulting merely from misperception or ignorance (as in Niemi's study). These data are presented merely to show how any bias involved in the recall of this particular generation (or any other group) can be expected to be largely self-cancelling.

Slightly reassured about the validity of the figures presented in table 11, we can return to an examination of them. Of the younger generation, 8.4 percent were Democrats at the time of the realignment but had come from Republican families; this was nearly balanced, however, by the 5.9 percent from Democratic families who took on a Republican identification on entering the electorate—leaving only a small net gain for the Democrats from this source. Table 13 summarizes the inter-

Table 13	Sources of Increase in Democratic Strength between Generations		
Alternative (parental) position:	Movements toward Democrats	Movements away from Democrats	Net
Republican	8.4	5.9	2.5
No partisanship	13.0	4.3	8.7
	21.4	10.2	11.2

generational movements toward and away from the Democrats and makes clear the importance of nonpartisan families, rather than Republican ones, as the source of new Democrats. Thirteen percent of this "New Deal generation" were Democrats whose father had identified with neither of the major parties; only 4.3 percent followed the opposite path. The net gain for the Democrats from this source is substantial: it can be calculated, in fact, that 78 percent of the intergenerational Democratic increase came from nonpartisan or nonpolitical families.

It thus may be unnecessary to posit misperception or even much of a decline in the ability of parents to pass their partisanship on to their offspring in order to account for the Democratic leanings of the new cohorts. (In fact, proportionately many more of the young Republicans came from Democratic homes than the other way around. This is due to the larger number of Democratic parents, of course; looked at another way, the Democratic parents were somewhat more successful than the Republicans at socializing their children; still, about 60 percent of the children of Republican families remained Republicans.) Not the children of Republicans, but the children of immigrants, independents, minor party supporters, and "potential" Democrats, as well as the children of established Democrats, appear to have made up the youthful component of the New Deal coalition.

Six

The Revolt of the City

> The really revolutionary surge behind the New Deal lay in this coupling of the depression with the rise of a new generation, which had been malnourished on the congestion of our cities and the abuses of industrialism. Roosevelt did not start this revolt of the city. What he did do was to awaken the climbing urban masses to a consciousness of the power in their numbers.[1]

The changes in party fortunes that took place in the twenties and thirties, which Lubell explains in large part as a "revolt of the cities," will be examined here in the context of one particular city, Chicago. There are two reasons for attempting to expand in this way the rather tentative hypotheses about the dynamics of the realignment.

The immigrant-filled, industrial cities of the Northeast and the Midwest have long been recognized as the keystones of the New Deal coalition. Certainly demographic differences and especially political differences affected the responses of the urban voters during this period (New York was a Democratic city that became much more solidly so; in Philadelphia, where Republicans were strong, the Democratic coalition took longer to build). But as one observer of Chicago ethnic politics said of the period, "given the variations in the political and ethnic makeup of American cities, the similarities in their political development are a good deal more striking than the differences."[2] Chicago, then, though its own political peculiarities will certainly be taken into account, can be regarded usefully as a case study representative of the larger social and political processes occurring simultaneously in many other cities. In a study of Chicago politics written in 1929, in fact, Merriam justifies his efforts precisely on the grounds that "Chicago has been and continued to be the most typically American city of the . . . larger municipalities. No other community is more closely allied with the combined growth of rail and waterways, of agriculture and manufacturing."[3]

Aside from the substantive merits of such an investigation, a case study, especially that portion of it based on the analysis of precincts, allows one to escape some of the pitfalls of ecological analysis. The patterns already found on a national level (chap. 2), among large groups of cities, or even on a county level, could be masking a number of contradictory individual shifts. Though they seem to support the contention that the realignment was based more on mobilization than on conversion, such an inference would be unwise. As one moves down to smaller units of analysis, however, the danger of succumbing to the ecological fallacy is lessened. This occurs because we can couch our interpretations of the aggregate trends in a sounder knowledge of the partisan movements which are likely to occur in the area (and which might well be obscured by analyzing units rather than individuals).

Some Inferences about
Voting Behavior

In 1920, Chicagoans gave 59 percent of their vote for governor to Republican Len Small, who was elected. Sixteen years later, they voted in almost exactly the same proportion for Horner, the Democratic gubernatorial candidate. As Converse aptly illustrates, there are many possible interpretations of such a situation, in which our knowledge extends only to the marginal vote totals in a pair of elections.[4] The easiest assumption to make, and one that satisfies both the Downsian model of vote choice and notions of the stability of party identifications, is the "assumption of minimal change." In this case we would assume that of the Republicans' 59 percent support in the first election, 19 percent was shifted into the Democratic camp in the second election. Such an interpretation provides considerable reduction in complexity but may well be at odds with reality: "there remains a wide range of possible change patterns that would attest to some continuity of behavior and yet would involve much more gross change than is represented [by this assumption]."[5]

In this exercise Converse is, of course, using another device for reducing complexity: he assumes that the electorate consists of the same individuals each time. Many studies of aggregate voting data have made the same implicit assumption. But recognizing, as one certainly must if one is dealing with elections sixteen years apart, that the composition of the electorate changes, sometimes dramatically, from election to election, introduces both complexity and verisimilitude.

The four parts of figure 14 represent four pairs of elections. In each pair, the party with a 40 percent minority in the first election enjoys a 60 percent majority in the second election. The first pair (a) is Converse's assumption of minimal change: 20 of the 60 party Y supporters in the first election support the opposition in the second. As Converse points out, various other exchanges are compatible with these marginal shifts; it should be noted, however, that all possible interpretations of the change involve vote-switching in the electorate, which does not change in composition over the time considered.

Since this is almost never the case, the next three pairs, in which 60 new voters are added to the initial electorate of 100, are more in accord with reality. In the simplest of these situations, the second pair (b), new voters completely explain the increase in votes (from 40 to 100) received by party X. All of the partisans in the first election continue to support their party. This is, of course, highly simplistic and unlikely. The third pair (c) represents the other (even less likely) extreme. There is a complete transfer of support in this case between parties X and Y; the new voters accrue predominantly to X, but a few support party Y in the second election.

The fourth pair of elections (d) represents a more complex situation, one that is probably more likely to occur in the real world. Here the vote for party X in the second election is composed of 20 switchers from Y to X as well as "standpatters"

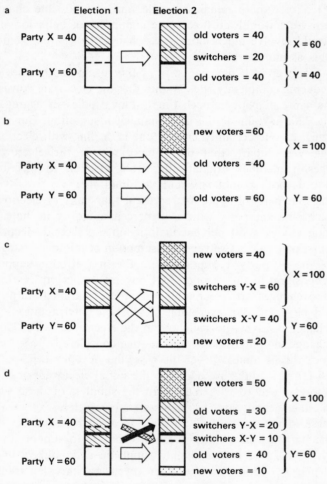

Figure 14   Patterns of electoral change

and the majority of the new voters. In addition, party Y's supporters in the second election, though predominantly the same
as in the first election, have also seen some changes: a few are
switchers from party X and some others are new voters.

Considering again the change in Chicago's gubernatorial vote
between 1920 and 1936, it is reasonable to assume that an accurate description of the change resides somewhere between
situations b and d. Most of the increased support for the Democrats came, perhaps, from new voters (both young people and
older citizens who may not have voted in 1920), but some
probably came from Republican converts or defectors as well.
This is, in effect, the "minimal change" assumption amended
to take new voters into account; but one cannot rule out the
possibility that some Democrat-to-Republican switching took
place within some areas in Chicago. The advantage of analyzing wards, and more particularly precincts, is this: if the
units analyzed are sufficiently homogeneous demographically,
the latter source of complexity can be virtually eliminated. In
an ethnic neighborhood which became progressively Democratic throughout the years in question, the amount of Democrat-to-Republican conversion is likely to be negligible—an
assumption which could not be made about the city as a whole.
This simplifying assumption will prove to be quite useful later.

A City of Immigrants

In 1930, two-thirds of Chicago's population
consisted of immigrants and their children—down from nearly
80 percent thirty years earlier. The city was home, in addition,
to 234,000 Negroes. All in all, native whites of native parentage constituted only 28 percent of Chicago's population. The
exceedingly ethnic nature of the city is supported by data on
religious affiliations; in 1936 Chicago contained 927,000 Catholics, 363,000 Jews, and only 505,000 Protestants.[6] Eleven
percent of Chicagoans were first or second generation Germans; a similar number were of Polish extraction and there
were almost the same number of Jews from various countries,
predominantly Russia. In order, the other major immigrant
groups were Italians, non-Jewish Russians, Swedes, and Czechs.

In addition, of course, there were thousands of second- and third-generation Irish, who by the calculations of the Census Bureau now fell within the purview of "native Americans," though we may doubt that they considered themselves as such. Chicago, like other northern cities, was characterized by areas of high ethnic concentrations, neighborhoods which lay mostly in a ring, part way between the Loop and the city's outer limits. This is Mike Royko's description of immigrant Chicago:

> The neighborhood-towns were part of larger ethnic states. To the north of the Loop was Germany. To the northwest was Poland. To the west were Italy and Israel. To the southwest were Bohemia and Lithuania. And to the south was Ireland. . . . In every neighborhood could be found all the ingredients of the small town: the local tavern, the funeral parlor, the bakery, the vegetable store, the butcher shop, the drugstore. . . . The borders of the neighborhoods were the main streets, railroad tracks, branches of the Chicago River, branches of the branches, strips of industry, parks, and anything else that could be glared across.[7]

By the 1920s the flow of newcomers had ceased. From 1900 to 1910 the foreign-born white population increased by a third, from 1910 to 1920 by only 3 percent. The Dillingham percentum plan and the 3 percent quota operated to restrict immigration from southern Europe, and the 1924 plan was even more restrictive, based on 2 percent of the population in 1890 instead of 3 percent in 1910. The immigrants had found jobs, in the packinghouses and steel mills and thousands of smaller industries in Chicago and were settled into their ethnic enclaves by the mid twenties. But integration into the economy preceded integration into the polity. A study of the naturalization process indicates that there was generally about an eleven-year period between arrival in the United States and filing of first papers.[8] The great majority of Poles, Lithuanians, Italians, Yugoslavs, Russians, and Czechs who settled in Chicago arrived after 1900, many of them well after. The peak years of immigration for these groups, in fact, were around 1905–13; the majority of these newer immigrant groups probably were not even able to vote until after the First World War. In 1930 over 70 percent

of the older ethnic groups—Irish, Swedes, Germans, and Nor-
wegians—were naturalized, but only about half the Czechs and
Russians and a third of the Poles and Italians, and 25 percent
of the Lithuanians.[9] Clearly there existed the potential for a
massive increase in ethnic political participation—and possibly
ethnic political "clout"—in the mid twenties.

Lubell maintained that the influx of immigrants around the
turn of the century and their high birth rates presaged a national political upheaval sometime in the late twenties or early
thirties. An examination of population figures for Chicago
might have led one to predict that some changes would occur
in that city as well. In a Polish area on the near northwest side,
for example, 30 percent of the population was first-generation
immigrants in 1930, and 48 percent of the inhabitants were the
children of Polish immigrants. Comparing these latter groups
with their counterparts in the neighborhood who had native-
born parents, one finds the second-generation Poles to be much
more concentrated in the younger age groups. Only 17 percent
of the native-parentage people were between the ages of 18
and 29, while a quarter of those with foreign or mixed parentage fell into this age group, the age groups that had recently
attained political majority or would do so within the next few
years. The concentration of people in their teens and twenties
(in about 1930) within these ethnic neighborhoods is quite striking. These two factors, naturalization and demography, explain
why the votes cast in these neighborhoods increased in the
1920s and 1930s even as their populations declined.

The Political Background

Merriam described city politics, generically, as
being completely separate in substance from national politics.[10]
The behavior and positions of the national Republicans and
Democrats have been discussed briefly above, particularly as
they related to the groups with which we are most concerned:
those who eventually created a Democratic majority. What were
the characteristics of the local Chicago parties at the time which
might have counteracted or reinforced these national images?

Chicago politics before 1928, like Chicago's neighborhoods, can best be described as feudal, and the political behavior of Chicago's ethnic groups during that period can best be termed inconsistent. The two are not unrelated: the same sociodemographic processes, political events, and personalities that forged a more centrally organized Democratic machine created a new and long-lasting alliance among the various immigrant groups.

Chicago Republicans during the early years of the twentieth century suffered somewhat more from factionalism than did Democrats. In 1929 Merriam identified three powerful Republican factions that had persisted for some years, all of them centered around individuals rather than policies, all perfectly capable of supporting Democratic candidates to enhance their position vis-à-vis their rivals. Factions seemed to generate more of the same: the original organizer of the faction behind Mayor Thompson defected in 1923 to join the rival Republican group headed by the governor.[11] "Big Bill" Thompson, mayor from 1915 to 1923 and from 1927 to 1931, was, until his defeat in 1931, the party's most consistent vote-getter among nearly all groups in the city, even those that tended to vote Democratic for other offices. Aside from Thompson's very impolitic behavior toward the end of his reign—he began sounding extremely xenophobic—perhaps most important in the long run is the fact that he was not sufficiently concerned with building a strong machine based on stable coalitions. By the late twenties, Thompson had alienated enough Republican leaders to undercut his strength enormously. His last remaining bastion of support was the Black Belt, but in the 1930 election he proved himself overconfident of the blacks' unstinting loyalty when he endorsed the Democratic senatorial candidate against the Republicans' Ruth Hanna McCormick. This attempt backfired: Thompson was denounced by many Negro leaders, and Mrs. McCormick received 76 percent of the black vote. Scandals associated with Thompson's administration in 1927, 1928, and 1930 further weakened his vote-getting ability and damaged Republican strength generally.

There had been, meanwhile, two predominant factions in the Democratic party, one which might be described as primarily Irish and spoils-oriented, the other mildly reformist. The Irish faction had succeeded to leadership by the twenties, and in general the Democrats were relatively more united than the Republicans during this period. The gradual displacement of the Irish hold by the forces united around Anthony Cermak, who was eventually elected mayor in 1931, provided the Democrats with the means to forge a strong ethnic-based coalition. Cermak and his allies took advantage of what was perhaps the single most important issue to many of Chicago's nonnative citizens: Prohibition. The United Societies for Local Self-Government, formed in 1906, became Chicago's chief anti-Prohibition organization. More important,

> as time went by it became rather pro-Democratic, particularly because most Chicago anti-Prohibitionists were Democrats, and primarily because Anton Cermak was its secretary and leading figure and used the organization for his own and and his party's success. The United Societies was the outstanding interethnic . . . organization in the city; it continued to exist and derived its power from the fact that the overwhelming majority of Chicago's ethnics found the idea and then the actuality of Prohibition absolutely repugnant.[12]

And on other issues salient in the ethnic neighborhoods of Chicago, while Thompson was beginning to sound more and more nativistic, the local Democrats were speaking out in the immigrants' interests. When a joint Slavic committee was formed in 1927 to oppose immigration restriction, Cermak was temporary president. And the Chicago delegation testifying against the Johnson Act (which based immigration quotas on the 1890 census) was led by Alderman Jacob Arvey and Congressman Adolph Sabath, both Democrats.

Still, until the late 1920s, both parties often appeared to be collections of warring factions, more concerned with infighting than with issues. The ethnic response to this political imbroglio is not surprising: most of the largest ethnic groups in Chicago adhered consistently and at all levels to neither the Democrats nor the Republicans prior to 1928. "The newcomers' political allegiance goes first to those human beings who satisfy his immediate and urgent needs,"[13] and so the newer immigrants in particular tended to be volatile in their voting behavior. Soci-

alization producing an enduring "party identification" among
these groups took place only gradually. An interesting indication of this is the extent to which the older immigrant groups
—Swedes and Germans—showed a consistency in their voting behavior across several offices, while the new immigrants'
voting patterns were less uniform. Allswang suggests that the
Swedes and Germans were by this time more "party-oriented,"
while the vote of the newer groups was still influenced by personalities, and perhaps issues, rather than a long-term party
commitment.[14] Members of the newer groups, in the terminology used here, were not yet immunized: they did not yet
have a strong and consistent partisan attachment.

In general, the immigrant-stock areas of Chicago were somewhat more Democratic than the rest of the city, and more Democratic in local elections than in national.[15] There were some
differences, of course, among various nationalities. These differences, as well as the volatility of ethnic voting behavior, can
be illustrated by a brief description of the votes of the nine
ethnic groups that Allswang studied in the elections from 1918
to 1932. In 1918 Wilson's appeal had not yet soured, and all
the newer immigrant groups voted Democratic for senator, congressman, and sheriff; this carried over into the mayoral election of 1919. The Germans, Swedes, Jews, and Negroes tended
to vote Republican. In 1920 the "tenuousness of newer immigrant Democratic loyalty became apparent"[16] and only the
Lithuanians were left supporting the Democratic ticket. This
pattern persisted in the 1924 national elections and in the 1927
mayoral elections, when Thompson did well among all groups,
losing only among the Czechs, Poles, and Lithuanians, and then
only by a small margin. In 1928, all this changed. Al Smith and
Tony Cermak led the Democratic ticket to an impressive victory among all the groups except Swedes and blacks. The former moved into the Democratic column in the elections of
1930, the latter not until 1936 at least.[17] The clearest change
in the ethnics' voting behavior was at the presidential level,
since on a local level many of the groups had been mildly (and
erratically) Democratic before 1928. Between 1928 and 1936
Chicago politics were "nationalized." Loyalty to the local Democrats (or Republicans) went along with loyalty to the national

parties more often than it had before, and there was more con-
tact between local leaders, such as Cermak, and the national
party (brought about at least partially by the growing welfare
functions of the national government and the resulting neces-
sity of currying favor with the national party leaders).

The question remains to be answered which of the many possible patterns of change (some of which are summarized in
fig. 14) account for this convincing emergence of Democratic
loyalty among Chicago's immigrant-stock citizens. Though analyses such as those of Allswang and Gosnell lucidly describe the
change in Chicago voting patterns, they may leave the impression that heretofore loyal Republicans among Jews, Italians,
Yugoslavs, Germans, and other groups were permanently con-
verted to the Democratic party during this period. Some undoubtedly were; immigrants and their children could not be
expected to have party loyalties as immutable as those of na-
tives. But we should keep in mind that the Chicago electorate
of 1936 was very different and quite a bit larger than that of
1920. Votes cast in the presidential election increased by well
over 100 percent, far over the rate of growth of the adult population—and the additions, one can assume, were young citizens, those newly naturalized, and those who did not vote in
the 1920s. (The latter group probably overlapped considerably
with the first two.) These were the additions to the electorate
which, it is argued, gave the Democrats an advantage after 1928.

Studying the Voting Behavior
of Chicago Wards

Examining the voting behavior during this pe-
riod within Chicago wards offers itself as a useful way to study
the progress of the realignment. Electorates of 60,000 rather
than 2,000,000, about which some population data is available, make the task of inferring individual change (or stability) from aggregate trends somewhat easier; and the existence
of a number of such units over time makes it possible to use
correlation analysis to identify the changing bases of party support in terms of the past voting behavior of the wards and their
ethnic composition.

At least two major problems inhere in this approach, however. First, the ward boundaries, with some exceptions, were
not coterminous with neighborhood and, therefore, ethnic divisions. Far from a mere coincidence, this fact represents the
effort that the native-stock and the Irish politicians of both
parties made to dilute the potential power of the newer immigrants. Gosnell remarks upon "the extent to which nationality and racial groups were cut into small bits by the 1921
and 1931 ward lines. Ward committeemen of Irish extraction
have been particularly active in splitting up their bailiwicks so
as to prevent their defeat by Italian, Polish or Jewish rivals."[18]
Of course this situation confirms the notion that before the late
1920s, though both parties received support from the recent
immigrants, neither allowed them to share in power. The bind-
ing nature of a group's loyalty to a party has much to do with
the initial perception that the party's actions benefit the group,
and one of the clearest symbols of such benefit is the appear-
ance of Polish or Jewish or Italian names on the roster of party
leadership. Such appearances were all too rare before the late
1920s. In short, while the gerrymandering inflicted on Chicago
wards makes it difficult to draw conclusions about ethnic voting, it makes a significant point about the political positions of
ethnic groups.

Since the ward committeemen had always to keep one step
ahead of their potential rivals, and since the wards must be
redrawn after each decennial census, the boundaries underwent
a change during the period of our analysis. This is the second
problem involved in analyzing voting behavior by wards. Half
of the fifty wards remained virtually identical when the ward
lines were redrawn in 1931 on the basis of the 1930 census.
For others, roughly equivalent areas can be arrived at by in-
specting ward maps (figs. 15 and 16) and specifications of ward
boundaries, and then grouping wards. Thus the 17th ward and
the 19th ward had their boundaries altered in 1931 to the point
where they cannot be regarded as comparable units over time.
However, if the two are combined, the area included in each of
the two time periods is similar. In this way, thirty-five groups
of wards can be created. Of the 1921 wards, twenty-six can be
carried over to the 1930s as single wards; one becomes two

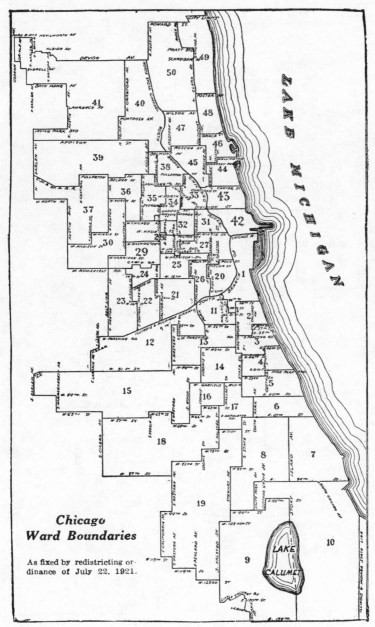

Figure 15   Chicago ward boundaries, 1921–30

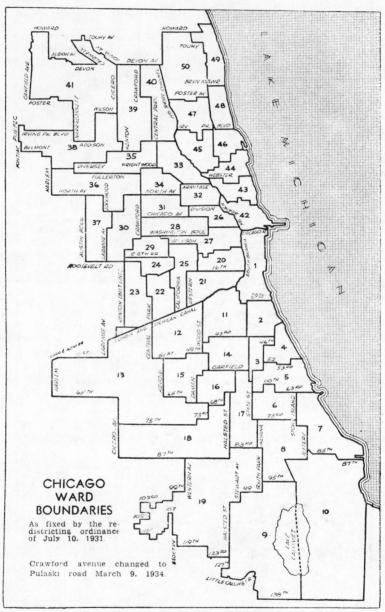

Figure 16　　　Chicago ward boundaries, 1931–40

wards in the next redrawing; six are in groupings of two wards; and equivalent areas for eight of the 1921 wards can be found only by combining them in groups of four. This method is necessarily quite inexact, since absolute areal equivalence was sacrificed in the interest of including all wards. (An alternative would have been to include only those units that did not change at all or changed only minimally; not only would this reduce the number of cases for analysis, but it may well have built in a political bias, given the motivations for redrawing ward lines discussed above.) Looking at voting patterns of precincts rather than wards would, of course, enable one to isolate more nearly identical geographical units over time, but the amount of work involved (the precinct boundaries are also redrawn) and the impossibility of obtaining demographic data for such areas make the present method more desirable. Table 14 presents the wards and groups of wards used in the analysis. Figure 17 shows, for comparative purposes, the ethnic makeup of the city according to the 1930 census.

Table 14   Chicago Ward Equivalences

1921	1931	Group No.	1921	1931	Group No.
1	1	1	27, 28, 31, 32	26, 27, 28	19
2	2	2	33	32	20
3, 4	3, 4	3	30, 37	30, 36, 37	21
5	5	4	40	40	22
6, 7, 8	6, 7, 8	5	41	39, 41	23
9	9	6	42	42	24
10	10	7	43	43	25
11, 12, 13, 15	11, 12, 13, 15	8	38	33	26
14	14	9	34, 35, 36	31, 34	27
16	16	10	39	35, 38	28
18	18	11	44	44	29
17, 19	17, 19	12	45	45	30
25	25	13	46	46	31
20, 21, 26	20, 21	14	47	47	32
22	22	15	48	48	33
23	23	16	49	49	34
24	24	17	50	50	35
29	29	18			

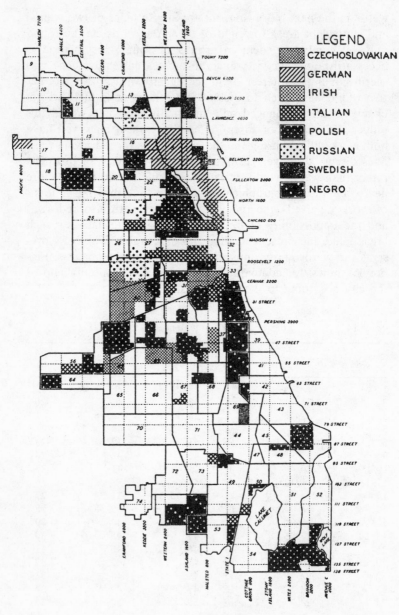

Figure 17   Ethnic groups in Chicago, 1930 (distribution in Community Areas)

The usual ways of examining the voting behavior of political units—whether they are states, counties, cities, or urban subdivisions, as in the present instance—over time, particularly when one is trying to describe or explain a period of realignment, involve first, a presentation in tabular or graphic form of the percentage of the two-party (or sometimes three-party) vote received by one of the parties in a series of elections. The classic example of this is V. O. Key's portrayal of the 1928–36 realignment in New England towns by displaying the proportion of the votes received by the Democrats in various types of towns.[19] Second, correlations between the percentage of the two-party vote given to, say, the Democrats at various times by particular political units are often used, in particular to identify "critical" elections (by this method, ones in which the vote correlates highly with the following elections but not with the preceding elections).

The base in both cases is the total vote or sometimes the two-party vote, which for our purposes is problematic. Thus the first method of analysis, percentaging the vote over time (which is relied upon heavily by Sundquist, among others), can answer only the simplest (if perhaps the most crucial) questions of who won, where, and when. Correlation analysis based on the two- or *n*-party vote can in addition pinpoint changes in party fortunes and identify critical elections, periods of gradual or secular realignment, and so forth. The question with which we are concerned, however—*how* did the Democrats win?—cannot be adequately answered by these means. If the Democrats came to power through their ability to channel an expanding electorate, the available voting population rather than just the voters must be the principal focus of analysis. In this way (allowing, of course, for the caveats that should always accompany ecological analysis) the source of the increase in Democratic strength—Republicans, third-party voters, nonvoters, or some combination of these—can be determined.

Patterns of Voting, 1924–40

The difference that results from using the available electorate rather than the voters as a base should become clearer in the next few pages. Table 15 uses the latter; in it are

Table 15   Democratic Percentage of Two-Party Presidential
                      Vote for Selected Wards, 1924–40

Election Year	Immigrant Wards	Middle Class Wards	Black Wards
1924	38	17	8
1928	60	26	30
1932	71	48	24
1936	81	53	48
1940	76	42	48

presented the Democratic percentage of the two-party vote in three areas, chosen because they typify black, native, and immigrant voting patterns throughout Chicago. They include the six wards, or groups of wards, with the highest foreign-born population; two middle-class, lakefront, predominantly native-born wards; and a ward that was (and is) largely black (92 percent in 1940). Three distinct patterns are apparent. The more ethnic wards (all had at least 27 percent foreign-born in 1940, and therefore the proportion of first- and second-generation immigrant-stock was likely to be 70 to 80 percent) gave more of their vote to Davis in 1924 than the native and black wards but still voted overwhelmingly Republican (the Democratic share of their three-party vote was only 29 percent; La Follette received 36,150 votes to Davis's 42,661). The big change in ethnic voting patterns came between 1924 and 1928: in the latter year these areas gave three-fifths of their vote to Al Smith, a proportion which increased, though not so dramatically, in both 1932 and 1936. But it is clear that the key Democratic advantage was gained in the 1928 election.

The native wards (each recorded 16 percent foreign born in 1940) were affected as well by Smith's candidacy, it appears, but the biggest jump in the Democratic vote came in 1932, in all probability as a protest vote against Hoover. By 1940 the Democratic percentage in these two wards had fallen below 50 percent, where it remained for a number of succeeding presidential elections.

Among black voters in the 2d ward Smith did well in relation to the 1924 Democratic vote, but still received only 30 percent of the two-party vote. In contrast to the other two groups, black voters showed the biggest increase in Democratic presidential voting in 1936. One can argue that in contrast to the native-stock protest vote, this should be seen as a gesture of approval of the Roosevelt administration's policies. However, even by 1940 the 2d ward had not yet gone solidly into the Democratic column.

In sum, from the figures in table 15, it appears that the timing of the realignment was somewhat different in different areas of the city: for immigrant-stock wards, the 1928 election was the most critical; for the native wards 1932 perhaps played this role, though the Democratic voting during the Depression may have represented in part defection from a Republican habit later resumed; and for the black 2d ward, 1936 seems to have been most important in ending the traditional Republicanism of the ward.

The conclusions to be drawn from these figures are nonetheless limited. Most importantly, nonvoters are ignored: 50 percent of the vote in a given ward or area could represent anywhere from 10 percent to 50 percent of the eligible electorate, depending on the turnout in that election. In the 1920s in particular, turnout in all elections, even presidential contests, was low almost everywhere, and particularly so among urban immigrant groups. If Republican victories among these groups in the twenties, in Chicago and elsewhere, were achieved with only a small proportion of the available electorate casting ballots, this in itself would say something important about the likely source of Democratic increases.

In other words, the *potential electorate* must be used as a base from which to calculate changing party strength. Once again we are presented with some methodological problems. The potential electorate includes both the naturalized and the nonnaturalized, the registered and the unregistered. These attributes can be seen as the result of political decisions; like the decision to vote or not to vote, they are affected by the candidates, issues, and campaigns at a particular time. That a greater proportion of Chicago's foreign-born residents were naturalized in 1932 than in 1920 and that more were registered in 1936 than in 1924 are facts that should not be ignored by considering only the actual electorate (i.e., those voting) but that should be taken carefully into account.[20] In some sense this provides us with a more "lenient" definition of the electorate—all those inhabitants of a ward who are twenty-one or over—and one might expect that the difficulty of ascertaining the size of the potential electorate would be correspondingly reduced. Unfortunately this is not the case, thanks to some inconvenient quirks in the census data. Through the fourteenth census (1920), data for the city of Chicago were presented by wards (as well as by census tracts). In the 1920s, however, members of the Chicago School of sociology at the University of Chicago undertook extensive studies of various neighborhoods in the city and ultimately evolved an exhaustive classification of the city according to Community Areas.[21] These areas were arrived at with an eye to the inhabitants' perceptions and definitions of their neighborhoods. The Census Bureau was sufficiently convinced of the merits of this method of subdividing the city that, from 1930 on, data for the city were presented principally according to Community Areas. In 1940, luckily for the present study, there was some reporting by wards; but in 1930, a year obviously of crucial interest, almost all population statistics are given only for the Community Areas, and it should be obvious by now that a classification that purported to take traditional ethnic and neighborhood ties into account would be at great odds with the arrangement of Chicago's political subdivisions. Even had this system not been in effect, of course, the fact that immediately upon the publication of the results of the 1930 census many of the wards they described were altered beyond recognition would render quite difficult the apparently simple task of establishing the size of the potential electorate in each ward.

As a result, the estimation of the potential electorate in each ward at five points in time between 1924 and 1940 is unavoidably rather crude. Reports or estimations of the *total* population by ward are available for 1924, 1930, 1936, and 1940, but a report of the population twenty-one and over exists only for 1940. Thus the potential electorate in each ward is calculated as the percentage of the total population that was twenty-one and over in 1940. The demography of the city certainly may have changed somewhat, but this method takes into account at least the gross differences in age distributions between, for example, foreign-stock and native-stock wards.[22]

In figures 18, 19, and 20 the percentages represent the Democratic votes, Republican votes, and third-party votes as a proportion of the total potential electorate. The difference between

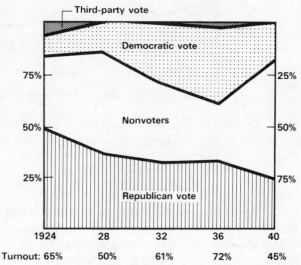

Figure 18   Democratic, Republican, and third-party presidential voters and nonvoters as proportions of the total electorate, in native, middle-class wards

the total number of votes cast and the number in the potential electorate provides the proportion of nonvoters in the ward. It should be obvious that while the differences in the *timing* of the Democratic increase discussed above can be seen in these figures also, they provide, additionally, significant information about the *sources* of the increase, which is lacking in table 15.

In none of the three areas described in these figures—which are the same areas as those in the preceding table—is the decrease in the Republican share of the electorate nearly as dramatic as the increase in the Democrats' share. More variable

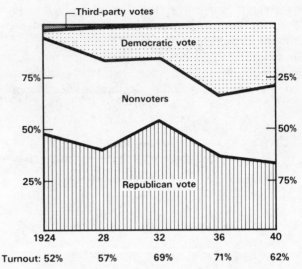

Figure 19   Democratic, Republican, and third-party presidential voters and nonvoters as proportions of the total electorate in a black (2d) ward

than the Republican vote—stated as a percentage of the total potential electorate—is the proportion of nonvoters. The Democratic party made its gains not so much at the expense of the Republican party as by mobilizing the nonvoting population; this is most clearly the case in the wards with the highest foreign-born populations, where the Republican proportion of the electorate shows almost no variation.

In the two lakefront native wards (fig. 18) the Republican vote, substantial both at the beginning and the end of the period, declined very gradually from 1924 to 1940. This pattern is consistent with the idea that the Republicans did not lose great numbers of regular supporters or identifiers but did fail to recruit new voters, and this interpretation in turn is compatible with the conclusions drawn in the previous chapter about the processes of partisan socialization at work during this period. It is interesting to note, however, that during the period between the elections of 1928 and 1936, when the major reshuffling of votes and partisanship is commonly supposed to have taken place, the Republican share of the electorate decreased by only four percentage points; the large increase in the Democratic vote (from 13 percent of the electorate to 37 percent) was accompanied by a corresponding rise in turnout —from 50 percent to 72 percent. Similarly, the decrease in the Democratic vote in 1940 was due not to desertion to the Republicans but, apparently, to abstention by those who had voted Democratic in the previous two elections.

Turnout in the black 2d ward, as in the lakefront native-stock wards, peaked in the second Roosevelt election (though it was high in 1932 as well) and dropped again in 1940. A notable change took place between 1932 and 1936 in which Democrats more than doubled their share of the electorate, from 16 percent to 34 percent, and the Republicans' portion declined from 52 percent to 37 percent. This appears on the surface, at least, to be an instance of real change in preferences

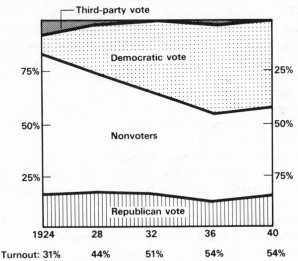

Figure 20   Democratic, Republican, and third-party presidential voters and nonvoters as proportions of the total electorate in wards with highest percent foreign-born

on the part of individual voters. The turnout rates in these
two presidential elections were nearly identical. Of course dis-
gruntled Republicans could have sat out the 1936 election while
heretofore apathetic residents of the 2d ward cast a vote of af-
firmation for FDR. But the magnitude of the change implies a
good deal of individual change—something not found in either
the native or ethnic white neighborhoods.[23] The black neighborhoods were always fairly well organized by the Republicans
and were quite consistently loyal to Thompson in particular.
But the social and economic position of most people in the 2d
ward was such that they could not easily afford political loyalties which no longer provided material benefits. In 1931
Thompson had been defeated by Cermak (despite black support); by 1936 the Kelly-Nash machine, which succeeded to
party leadership after Cermak's assassination in 1933, was
firmly in control of most of Chicago's patronage. We may
hypothesize that between 1932 and 1936, the Democratic organization, by virtue of its new position, would have been able
to make substantial inroads into the black community.[24]

It is the predominantly foreign-stock wards on which our
attention should focus as on a representation in miniature of
the emerging urban, industrial, immigrant masses, which in one
way or another provided the foundation of the new Democratic
majority. But in what way? How, precisely, was this new majority built: on the strength of Republican disillusion, or with the
support of the previously uncommitted? The pattern of voting
in the six foreign-stock wards is one of stability of the Republican vote alongside a substantial increase in turnout and in the
Democratic vote.[25] Unlike the native and black wards described
by figures 18 and 19, the growth in the Democratic vote does
not vacillate and seems to be accounted for almost completely
by the equally steady growth in the proportion of the available
electorate that voted in the presidential elections. While turnout
levels never reached the heights they do in the other wards, the
increase is more impressive. The contrast between 1924, a very
Republican year for Chicago ethnic groups, and 1940 is striking.[26] As can be seen from table 15, the Democratic presidential vote was 38 percent of the two-party vote in 1924 and 76

percent in 1940: a change of amazing magnitude. Yet figure 20 suggests strongly that this change took place with very little change in the overall Republican strength in these neighborhoods. Fifteen percent of what we estimate to constitute the electorate in 1924 voted for the GOP; thirteen percent did so in 1940. The difference, of course, is that while in 1924 less than a third of the electorate voted, in 1940, 50 percent did so—and those additional participants voted for the Democrats.

In this context it should be noted that while an estimated 71 percent of the adult population in the native lakefront wards (see fig. 18) was registered to vote in 1924, that figure for the ethnic neighborhoods represented in figure 20 was only 35 percent. What does this say about the nature of voting and nonvoting in these and similar parts of Chicago? Most relevant is the fact that nonvoters in the immigrant areas in the mid twenties were more likely to be "habitual" nonvoters, while nonvoting in areas of relatively high registration may have denoted simply a lack of interest in or concern with a particular election.[27] Lack of widespread party identification can more easily be equated with nonregistration and habitual nonvoting than with periodic nonvoting when registration is relatively high. Thus the condition we have called nonimmunization was much more prevalent in the foreign-stock wards than in the native-stock wards, and the former areas were therefore much more susceptible to the appeals of what was essentially a "new" party: the Democrats in the 1930s.

Figures 21, 22, and 23 illustrate the ways in which the pattern we have found in these wards varies among the different ethnic groups. The Democratic percentage of the two-party vote changes similarly in the three areas, but the perspective afforded by considering nonvoters as well as voters shows three distinct patterns of change.

The 23d ward, occupied during this period by Czechs and a few Russians, suffered some decline in Republican voting (as a proportion of the total available electorate) but saw a much larger increase in the Democratic vote. From 1924 to 1928, for example, while the Republican vote changed only gradually, the Democratic vote was swelled, apparently, by the addition of

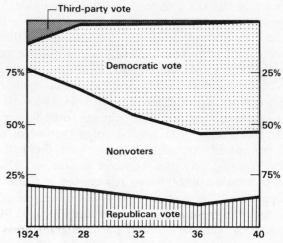

Figure 21   Democratic, Republican, and third-party presidential voters and nonvoters in an ethnic (Czech) ward

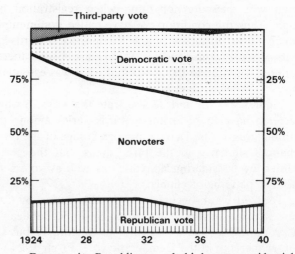

Figure 22   Democratic, Republican, and third-party presidential voters and nonvoters in an ethnic (Polish, Italian, Russian) ward

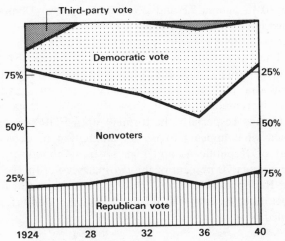

Figure 23   Democratic, Republican, and third-party presidential
voters and nonvoters in an ethnic (German) ward

those who had not voted in the previous election as well as by
those who had voted for La Follette. In 1932 and 1936 the
Republican vote, as might be expected, declined; but particularly between 1932 and 1936 the mobilization of nonvoters
appears to contribute the greater share to the Democratic surge.
By 1940, turnout in this West Side neighborhood, which had
been only 43 percent sixteen years previously, was up to two-
thirds of the potential electorate.

Much the same change in voting behavior took place in the
wards included in figure 22, which were at the time primarily
Polish and secondarily Italian. Turnout in these wards remained
fairly low; the major increase in turnout and in the Democratic
vote was between 1924 and 1928. La Follette voters appear to
have contributed to the Democratic victory here in 1928 as in
the Czech 23d Ward. The striking thing about the presidential
election returns from these typical immigrant "river wards" is
that the Republican share of the electorate remained virtually
the same from 1924 to 1940. If one is willing to assume that
the Republican voters were largely the same people from election to election, then it is clear that in wards such as those por-

trayed in figures 21 and 22, the increase in Democratic votes must have come from that portion of the electorate which had not voted in the earlier elections.

The North Side ward represented in figure 23 was home to many Germans, and it is clear that their voting behavior was somewhat different from that of more recent arrivals. Turnout here increased until 1936, benefiting both Democrats and Republicans (especially the former) until FDR's second election, when what appears to be a combination of defection on the part of Republicans and high levels of mobilization gave the Democrats 70 percent of the two-party vote. In 1940, however, the Republican vote was back up to a quarter of the available electorate, turnout had declined, and the Democratic vote declined with it.

Sources of the New Democratic Majority

Correlation coefficients have been used in a number of studies, usually to clarify the timing of realignments or to identify "critical elections." MacRae and Meldrum, in a study of critical elections in Illinois, advise that "all the elections before the reorientation should show high correlations with one another; all elections afterward should also be highly correlated; but any election before the critical transition should show a lesser correlation with any election afterward."[28] Indeed, Allswang's examination of the votes of nine ethnic groups appears to support the idea that 1928 was a critical election in Chicago, as the percent Democratic of the two-party vote in that year correlates more highly with the elections that follow than with the preceding elections.[29] Using a similar analysis Shover finds that 1928 was *not* a critical election in California.[30]

But this is a rather one-dimensional approach. It assumes that the choices confronted by the voters (the consistency of their choices over time being what is at issue in the correlation analysis) are two: Democratic or Republican (sometimes, as in 1924, the relevant choices are more numerous). The choice obscured by this perspective is that of not voting at all. The choice of nonvoting can be included in analysis of correlation coefficients by once again using as data the percentages the

Democratic and Republican votes were of the total available electorate. In this way, the Democratic and Republican votes can be correlated over time, as is generally done; in addition, Democratic and/or Republican voting in a given election can be correlated with nonvoting in that election or in an earlier or later election.

The inference which was drawn from the figures in the preceding section—that the composition as well as the size of the Republican vote remained basically unchanged throughout this period—is supported by the correlations in table 16. All the correlations are strong and significant. There is no election that

Table 16   Republican Voting in Chicago Wards: Correlation Coefficients over Time

	1928	1932	1936	1940
1924	.92	.86	.88	.67
1928		.90	.94	.76
1932			.93	.82
1936				.87

could be classified as "critical" for the Republicans (one virtue of this method of analysis is that a particular election can be found to be "critical" for one party and not the other, or that one party can be found to have realigned, but not the other). Elections closer together in time are correlated more highly than ones more distant from one another, but the locus of Republican support in Chicago did not change appreciably between 1924 and 1940.

For the Democrats (table 17) the picture is different. None of the correlations are as high as those in table 16, and there is a good deal less consistency among them. Clearly, the Democratic bases of support were more variable than the Republican. The Roosevelt-Landon election of 1936 stands out as something of an aberration—it correlates neither with those elections preceding it nor with the 1940 election. With this exception the basis of support for Democratic presidential candidates, while not as uniform as Republican support, shows no obvious period of change.

At the same time, a major difference between Republican and Democratic support is illustrated by the correlation between Republican and Democratic voting and nonvoting. Table 18 indicates clearly that nonvoting did not occur in the same areas which gave support to Republican presidential candidates.

Table 17   Democratic Voting in Chicago Wards: Correlation Coefficients over Time

	1928	1932	1936	1940
1924	.64	.78	.01	.55
1928		.71	.12	.55
1932			.24	.68
1936				.16

Table 18   Republican Voting and Nonvoting in Chicago Wards: Correlation Coefficients

		% Republican				
		1924	1928	1932	1936	1940
	1924	—.90	—.77	—.68	—.70	—.57
	1928		—.62	—.51	—.48	—.44
% Nonvoting	1932			—.59	—.47	—.50
	1936				—.56	—.40
	1940					.25

The correlation between Republican voting and nonvoting in 1924, for example, is —.90. Using 1924 as a base point—a year when turnout was low all over the city and the growth of the nonimmunized population was at its peak—we can see that the Republican vote in every succeeding election shows a strong negative correlation with nonvoting in 1924. The Republicans never were able to draw on the nonimmunized population but instead continued to receive support from a consistent "hard core" of Republican voters. The Democrats, in contrast, were able to fashion a coalition that drew heavily on nonparticipants. In 1924 there was no relationship between nonvoting and Democratic voting (as compared with the negative association for

Republican voting); but the Democratic presidential votes of 1928, 1932, and 1940 are positively related to nonvoting in 1924.

David Burner has reported that Al Smith's candidacy boosted turnout in immigrant stock areas where voting rates had been low.

> The massive immigration of 1900 to 1914 was apparently paying dividends in votes in 1928. Part of the explanation for Smith's strength in the immigrant cities . . . was an apparent rise in voting among Roman Catholic women. . . . Within heavily Italian census tracts . . . we find voting precincts where female registration rose by twenty-nine percent.[31]

The effect the campaign of 1928 had on ethnic voting rates in Chicago can easily be seen by comparing figures 18, 19, and 20. In the native-stock wards, turnout actually declined between 1924 and 1928. In the black second ward, the voting rate increased by 9.6 percent. In contrast, in the wards with a high percentage of foreign-born residents, turnout in the presidential election increased by 41.9 percent.

Merriam and Gosnell found in 1924 that the highest levels of habitual nonvoting existed in immigrant-stock neighborhoods; if added to this is the recognition that many in these areas, not being naturalized, were not even eligible to vote at that time, the association between the ethnic character of a neighborhood (or a city) and its level of nonvoting should be clear. In these ethnic, largely working class wards of Chicago and other northern industrial cities in the 1920s, the *potential* for a new political majority lay. Figure 24, which demonstrates this, plots two relationships: one between percent foreign-born and percent Democratic, the other between percent foreign-born and nonvoting. The former association, only mildly positive in 1924, increased markedly in 1928 and again in 1932. Once more the 1936 Democratic vote seems to have been much more widely and disparately distributed throughout the city than was true of the vote in either 1932 or 1940. Aside from this exception, however, in 1928 and after there is a clear association between the ethnicity of the ward and its support for the Democratic presidential candidate. In contrast, the ethnicity of Chicago

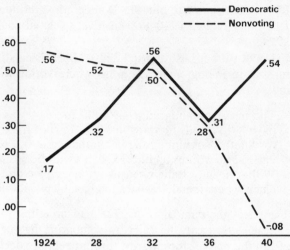

Figure 24   Correlation (Pearson r) of percent foreign-born with percent Democratic and with nonvoting, for Chicago wards

wards is increasingly less related to their turnout rates as one moves through this period, to the point that, by 1940, there is a slight negative correlation between percent foreign-born and percent of the electorate not voting. Meanwhile, a brief glance back at the coefficients in tables 19 and 20 shows that in the same year (1940) there is a slight positive association between Republicanism and nonvoting, while Democratic voting and nonvoting show a very strong negative relationship. All these findings indicate that by 1940 the new coalition had been solidified, and ethnic neighborhoods had been organized and mobilized by the Democrats.

Thus far in our case study of Chicago we have been discussing the electorate in various parts of Chicago without regard to age. The implication might be made, from the data presented in this chapter, that the Democratic gain was a result of the decision on the part of a good many adults who had declined to vote in the early twenties to support Smith and Roosevelt. Yet the retrospective survey data examined in the previous two chapters suggest that one of the primary sources of the growing Democratic strength in these years was the impressive support of the younger generation.

With voting returns aggregated on territorial bases such as wards there can, of course, be no direct test of the latter hypothesis. But one indirect possibility of measuring the impact of the "youth vote" offers itself. That is, one can investigate a possible association between the relative youthfulness of a ward and its vote. In the present case only a somewhat crude estimation of this trait—the percentage of the population twenty-one and over—was easily available. This varies among the 35 groups of wards from 62 percent to 89 percent and is at least an indication of the extent to which the ward is inhabited by older or younger citizens.

Table 20 presents the appropriate figures. A negative coefficient means that the party's voters tended to come from wards with a higher concentration of those under twenty-one and thus a higher concentration of new (and in general young) voters. All during the period between 1924 and 1940, the Republican vote shows a moderate positive correlation with the age of the

Table 19   Democratic Voting and Nonvoting in Chicago Wards: Correlation Coefficients

	% Democratic				
	1924	1928	1932	1936	1940
1924	—.02	.38	.23	.02	.46
1928		—.29	.07	—.10	.32
% Nonvoting 1932			—.17	—.13	.17
1936				—.74	.42
1940					—.77

Table 20   Correlation of Percent of Population 21 and Over with Republican and Democratic Voting

	1924	1928	1932	1936	1940
Republican	.31	.34	.20	.37	.23
Democratic	—.10	—.31	—.43	—.11	—.52

ward's inhabitants. Significantly, the Democratic vote shows an increasingly strong negative correlation (once again excepting 1936) with the percent twenty-one and over. (It should be noted that the age variable is not merely a surrogate for percent foreign-born: the two variables are insignificantly correlated at —.12.)

This is an indirect but convenient bit of data to support the contention that the Democratic majority was built partially with the support of millions of those voters who came of age in the late twenties and early thirties (many of whom were the children of immigrants) as well as on the mobilization of their heretofore nonparticipating elders.

The Dynamics of Partisan
Change: An Estimate

The innovative nature of the methods of analysis used in the preceding sections of this chapter lies in the fact that they take nonvoting into account, thereby providing a greater than usual amount of information about political behavior. Nonetheless, the major goal of this book is the understanding of the individual dynamics that underlie partisan change—and making inferences about these dynamics from aggregate data is always dangerous. Even though doubts about the validity of such inferences can appropriately be eased as one moves to smaller units of analysis, they can never be erased. As we know, Chicago's ward boundaries are not drawn to accord with natural ethnic or class divisions, and thus even voting patterns at the ward level may well hide complex interparty shifts among various groups within the ward.

One way to get around this is to analyze the votes of even smaller political units: precincts, preferably those so located as to be as socially homogeneous as possible. Happily, Allswang's study of Chicago provides the analyst with a painstakingly selected array of just such precincts. Allswang selected groups of census tracts that were ethnically pure; he then found precincts or groups of precincts within these areas whose boundaries did not change by more than two blocks between 1920 and 1936.[32] He concludes that he was "thus able to create a situation wherein I was dealing with the same ethnic group in the same political unit [over time]; and I could assume I was dealing with many of the same individuals throughout."[33]

Allswang points out that using dominance by one particular ethnic group as the initial criterion for selecting an area discriminates against the socioeconomically better-off members of the group, since they were less likely to live in such homogeneous areas. Because this has the effect of producing socioeconomically as well as ethnically homogeneous areas, it is ideally suited to the present analysis. Survey data from the past twenty years repeatedly inform us of the extent to which family, friends, work associates, and neighbors tend to vote similarly.[34] Obviously, there were some Republicans in these Chicago neighborhoods, but common sense tells us that in times of political change or crisis the general partisan movements of small, homogeneous areas would be in a single direction. This, at any rate, is the assumption made here, and it is an assumption that simplifies the task of untangling the kinds of changes going on during this period.

To visualize this simplifying process schematically, refer back to figure 14d. What we are able to do, in effect, is to eliminate the hatched arrow, which represents Democratic-to-Republican switchers. We assume that none of the habitual Democrats in these neighborhoods began to identify themselves as Republicans in the late 1920s and early 1930s. If one can then allocate the new voters between the parties and calculate how many Republican-to-Democratic "switchers" (the black arrow in fig. 14) are temporary defectors, the result is an approximation of the impact of partisan conversion in the Chicago version of the realignment.

In order to arrive at an estimate of conversion, we must find the difference between the *actual* Republican vote in these neighborhoods at the end of the period of realignment (1936) and the *predicted* Republican vote. Given the "no Democratic-to-Republican change" assumption, the predicted Republican vote would take into account mortality and recruitment of new voters and would allow for a certain amount of defection. It is summarized by the following formula:

$$R_{p2} = R_1 - mR_1 + r(V_2 - V_1) - dD_2$$

(where R = number of Republican votes, D = number of Democratic votes, V = total votes cast, m = expected mortality, r = expected recruitment of new voters, and d = expected [temporary] defection to Democrats).

The sources of these estimates are varied and undoubtedly questionable, but they are the best available. Assuming that the Republican identifiers were distributed in terms of age in approximately the same manner as the adult population, 19 percent of the 1920 Republican voters in these neighborhoods should have died by 1936.[35] The recruitment estimation is based on the 1952 SRC election survey. In that year, 535 of the respondents reported that they had first voted in the 1924, 1928, 1932, or 1936 election. Taking all these respondents together, the Republican vote is 33 percent. Among those with at least one foreign-born parent, the people with whom we are mainly concerned in this case study, the Republican percentage was only 26 percent. This latter figure is the one used to estimate the proportion of the new voters in these ethnic neighborhoods who became Republicans between 1920 and 1936. Finally, the estimated defection is based on an examination of a 1939 Gallup poll. In that survey, 14 percent of those who voted for Roosevelt in 1936 said that they were Republicans. Thus, 14 percent of the Democratic votes in 1936 are assumed to be Republicans who will eventually return to the fold.

If the predicted Republican vote minus the actual Republican vote in 1936 is stated as a proportion of the Democratic gain,

$$(R_{p2} - R_2)/D_2 - D_1$$

we can obtain an estimate of the amount of that increase due to permanent "conversion" of Republicans.

This formula is applied to the votes of four new immigrant groups, Czechs, Lithuanians, Yugoslavs, and Italians, and two older ones, Germans and Swedes. The results are presented in table 21. In no case is the bulk of the Democratic vote increase due to conversion, but there is an interesting distinction between the older and the more recent arrivals. Republicans among the latter seem to have undergone practically no conversion to Democratic identifications: once their mortality and their probable defection is taken into account, very little difference remains between the predicted and the actual 1936 Republican vote. This finding is congruent with the conclusion in the previous section, based on an analysis of the potential electorate. In figure 20, for example, a picture emerged of a small, stable Republican vote, which was overwhelmed by the Democratic tendencies of the former nonvoters. It would appear that in terms of individual behavior, most Republicans in these immigrant-stock areas maintained their party identification (though a few defected to vote for FDR), while some new voters, perhaps their children, came into the electorate as Republicans, making up for the natural attrition that would have occurred in the Republican ranks. Thus the growth of the Democratic strength is based on the support of an expanded electorate.

Table 21   Estimation of Change in Vote Resulting from Republican-Democratic Conversion in Chicago Ethnic Neighborhoods

Czechoslovak	11.5%	Italian	10.6%
Lithuanian	6.2	German	26.0
Yugoslav	3.6	Swedish	20.1

In the German and Swedish neighborhoods, the number of votes cast grew far less than in the precincts occupied by Czechs, Lithuanians, Yugoslavs, and Italians. This is natural, for two reasons: more of the Germans and Swedes were already citizens in the 1920s, and, having been citizens longer, they were both more prosperous and more integrated into the existing system of partisan divisions (the Republicanism of many German and Scandinavian families was, after all, a product of the Civil War and Reconstruction). As the condition of nonimmunization has been described, it was much less likely to exist among older immigrant groups. Thus with no great expansion in the electorate, conversion played proportionately a somewhat larger role, though certainly not a dominant one. And it should be noted that in figure 23, in a predominantly German ward, Republican voting was seen to decline temporarily in 1936 only to rise again in 1940; so it could be that temporary defection is a more important factor in these German and Swedish precincts than our formula would indicate.

Conclusion

The notion of party identification as political scientists now commonly use it gained currency at a time when explaining the remarkable stability of the party system seemed most important. No mechanism for dealing with large-scale aggregate partisan change is built into the model; thus what seem to be logical extensions of the model, should one ask it to deal with partisan change, have not been widely applied. One such extension is what I have called the mobilization of the non-immunized.

The process whereby large groups of disaffected or apathetic citizens are moved to take part in politics has usually been seen in rather apocalyptic terms by political scientists. McPhee himself uses the concept of nonimmunization to explain the Nazis' sudden rise to power.[1] Lipset and O'Lessker also make the argument that the Nazis received crucial support from new or nonimmunized voters.[2] In a recent article, Burnham analyzes pre-Weimar and Weimar voting patterns and concludes that the Nazi "contagion" touched primarily those who had previously supported the nonconfessional liberal and conservative parties as well as—or perhaps instead of—nonvoters.[3] But when he turns to a comparative examination of the sources of the Wallace vote in 1968, his chief concern is the ability of non-immunization (such as it is in the nonconfessional American environment) to forestall the rise of demagogues. "There is a widespread, not necessarily inaccurate, impression abroad to-day that some basic element within the system which has pro-tected American politics from a durably significant right-wing extremism has disappeared."[4] And in more general terms, Mil-brath suggests that "societies having large numbers of people who are intensely interested and active in politics . . . tend to have wide and deep conflicts which are very difficult to bridge."[5]

One may, however, concentrate on the less spectacular oper-ation of the mobilization cycle. Viewing it as a "cycle," in fact, rather than an extraordinary and even dangerous occurrence, provides for the processes of immunization and mobilization a place in the concept of "realignment" as it has been developed by political scientists. If realignment is an adjustment process, resynchronizing the party system with the realities of socioeco-nomic life, the spread of nonimmunization is a direct measure of the system's failure to articulate the demands of important groups in society, and as such it can be a harbinger of realign-ment. Realignment will not occur, of course, if the old cleav-ages are reinforced by new issues or reemphasized by attractive leaders.

But realignment can occur, and without much party-switch-ing on the part of those with established loyalties, if several con-ditions are met: (1) the nonimmunized share common needs or interests; (2) the old party alignment discourages the artic-ulation of these needs or interests; (3) a new alternative—new leaders in an old party, a new party altogether, an innovative platform—appears to provide a means by which the needs and interests of those previously outside the political system can be articulated within the partisan framework.

If this book has been successful, it has plausibly described the 1928–36 realignment in precisely these terms. But even given that the means of change in this particular instance in-volved more mobilization than conversion, is this process one which characterized other realignments in American history? Is it exportable—can it be used to analyze partisan change in other countries? Finally, might it tell us anything about the current period of "dealignment" and the future prospects of the American party system?

Nineteenth-Century Realignments

The realignment that saw the demise of the Whigs and the rise of the Republicans seems, on the surface, to be a poor candidate for an explanation based on mobilization. The question of slavery was undoubtedly a polarizing issue, one that generated enough deep-felt outrage on both sides to make plausible the idea that many people rejected their party on the basis of the party's stand on slavery. Sundquist argues that the Republicans drew much support from former Democrats.

> In Cincinnati, a thousand "unquestioned and adamantine" Democrats joined in calling an anti-Nebraska meeting; a Chicago gathering was led by Democrats who had previously supported Douglas. Democratic newspapers defected . . . At a . . . meeting in Ripon on March 20, the Republican party was born. "We went into the little meeting held in a schoolhouse Whigs, Free Soilers, and Democrats. We came out of it Republicans," wrote Alvin E. Bovay some years later.[6]

"The Democrats who switched to the Republican party," he concludes, "proved to be of sufficient number to make the new party the majority party in the North."[7]

The religious and ethnic cleavage that was solidified by this realignment pitted Democratic "liturgicals" against Republican "pietists." Included in the former group were Catholics, Irish and German, some German Lutherans, some Baptists. Among the pietists were numbered Congregationalists, Unitarians, Methodists, Presbyterians, and Scandinavian Lutherans.[8] Clearly, the mid nineteenth-century Protestant immigrants—the Germans and Scandinavians, many of whom arrived before the period of critical partisan change—would not have found much to attract them in either the Catholic-supported Democratic party or the rather nativist Whigs. In fact, in a political survey conducted in 1858 in Lansing, Michigan, proportionately more of the "doubtfuls"—those who could not reliably be classified as either Democrats or Republicans—were found among the young, the foreign born, and particularly the Germans, who were the most recent arrivals of the ethnic groups represented.[9] If being "doubtful" about party affiliation was, as seems probable, associated with nonvoting, the Lansing survey appears to be a small suggestion of the location of nonimmunized groups within the population. Furthermore, state voting patterns showing a stable Democratic vote and an expanding electorate (as the Republican party grew in strength) between 1840 and 1860, culminating in Republican victory, are strikingly similar to those of voting at the national and county levels in the 1920s and 1930s.[10] The implication, at least, is that the Republicans may have gained strength more from new voters (particularly immigrants) and third-party supporters than from Democratic losses. Finally, there is no reason the "polarizing" issue of slavery cannot be seen as well as a "mobilizing" issue, able to bring the previously uninvolved to the polls.

The 1896 realignment, which ushered in a long-lasting Republican hegemony, seems also—for quite a different reason—to be less than amenable to a "mobilization" explanation. The reason is that, in the years leading up to 1896, one is dealing with an electorate that was much more fully mobilized than that of the 1920s. Turnout in northern states did reach a peak in 1896, but according to Burnham's estimates, turnout was quite high (85.4 percent in nonsouthern states) in the years before the 1896 election.[11] Thus particularly in the North there was apparently not the growth of a free-floating citizenry like that which characterized the 1920s and, perhaps, the 1840s and 1850s. It may be that conversion, in this already mobilized electorate, played a greater role in the 1896 realignment. But two caveats are in order before drawing this conclusion. The first is that the process of "forgetting" had had plenty of time to operate. Younger voters in 1896 could be safely said to be, in Beck's terms, "children of normalcy"—neither they nor their parents had experienced, as adults, the polarizing events of mid century. Second, and perhaps more important, it has been amply documented that in the North, the pro-Republican forces emanated mainly from the cities.[12] The cities, of course, were the home of the newest citizens—the immigrants; and many cities, particularly in the Midwest, had doubled or tripled in size during the decade of the 1880s. Here is Degler describing the 1880s (a decade when, according to a "mobilization" scenario, the nonimmunized population should have been growing):

> In fact the number of immigrants who flooded into the country in that decade exceeded that of any other similar period in the century. Furthermore, those ten years were the seedtime of the city. . . . During that decade of transition neither the political parties nor the people were prepared by previous experience for the problems and nature of the new industrial, urban age.[13]

The results, in the 1890s, were that the industrial areas of the country became solidly Republican. "Taken together, the elections of 1894 and 1896 mark the emergence of the Republican party as the party of the rising cities."[14] Samuel Hays's discussion of the nature of Republican gains accords nicely with the idea that such emergence reflected Republican success at mobilizing the nonimmunized:

> The Republican gains of 1894, which continued over into 1896, were largely urban. The precise nature of this new strength is not yet clear, but it appears to have been composed largely of workers *and immigrants* who blamed the Democrats for the depression and who were suspicious of the economic interests and the nativist tinges of the farmers. [Italics mine.][15]

About both these periods one must necessarily be fairly speculative. Though careful analyses exist, particularly of the 1890s,[16] they have not examined the voting patterns with an eye to discovering the behavioral sources of the realignment, nor have they considered seriously the role of nonvoting in producing partisan change. Thus a good deal of careful research needs to be done to establish the relative predominance of mobilization and conversion in the nineteenth-century realignments.

Western Europe

Despite the clear differences between parties as institutions and, accordingly, in the nature of party identification in Western European countries on the one hand and the United States on the other,[17] several studies suggest that, cautiously applied, the notion of nonimmunization and mobilization as sources of partisan change is not limited in its utility to America.

Perhaps the most extensive analysis of this nature is to be found in Butler and Stokes' *Political Change in Britain*. Two findings in particular are quite similar to those in the present work. In trying to pinpoint the sources of the growth of the British Labour Party during the last half century, they investigate the transmission of party identification from generation to generation. Only a very small net gain has accrued to the Labour Party because of children from Conservative families rejecting their parents' party. There has been, not surprisingly, some movement from Liberal families to Labour support, but the authors conclude: "in every age cohort manual workers whose fathers were not remembered as having a partisan alignment were an important source of new strength for the Labour Party."[18] Second, Butler and Stokes found that even over the short run, processes of electoral replacement rather than conversion often played the key role. Only one-fifth of the Conservative decline between 1959 and 1963, for example, was due to "straight conversion between Conservative and Labour."[19] Replacement of the electorate was responsible for about a quarter of the Conservative gain: more of those who died were Conservatives, and the young, less "immunized" by previous voting experience, supported Labour disproportionately, just as the young in the 1930s supported the Democrats. The largest apparent source of change lay in differential turnout: "1959 nonvoters were much more likely to support Labour than Conservatives . . ." and presumably did so with their votes in 1963. In summarizing the total pro-Labour movement between 1959 and 1964, Butler and Stokes conclude that,

> The small net contribution of straight conversion to Labour serves as a salutory warning to anyone who automatically

interprets 'swing' simply as a direct and one-dimensional switch from one side to the other and not as the complex product of a large number of often contrary movements.[20]

Similar conclusions about the importance of electoral replacement (though not specifically mobilization of peripheral groups) in producing change are reached by Giacomo Sani in his recent studies of Italy. He calculates that about 12 percent of the 1975 electorate was new since 1972, and the party preferences of these younger citizens were skewed considerably to the Left. Thus despite the stability of party loyalties among most Italians, the Left (especially the Communist party) has gained by the fact that new electors of a different political stripe are replacing the older voters. He estimates that almost 60 percent of the Left parties' gains between 1972 and 1975, quite a short period, are due to generational change as opposed to shifts in voting choice. This situation represents in part a breakdown of the socialization or immunization process:

> there appears to be a discontinuity, or at least a gradual change in the distribution of partisan preferences that sets apart the different generations of voters. The mechanisms of political socialization apparently no longer produce among the young voters a distribution of party preferences that mirrors very closely, as it did in the past, the political orientations of the older cohorts.[21]

To take a different example: France, a country where partisan changes have been frequent and party attachments therefore somewhat ephemeral, has often been compared with the United States: "Where political parties are poorly organized, there fluctuations and trends in party support will be greatest . . . reflecting the inability of politicians to encapsulate support on a persisting basis."[22]

Inglehart and Hochstein, in their article comparing the U.S. and France in terms of party-system "alignment" and "dealignment," offer abundant evidence to show that the growth of Gaullism in the 1960s was based largely on the mobilization of nonimmunized citizens. Almost half the Gaullist gain came from those whose fathers had had no reported party identification; "voters whose fathers had supported parties of the Left accounted for less than 11 percent of the Gaullist vote."[23] The findings of resistance to change by those who have inherited a clear partisan preference, and of a good deal of change produced by those from nonpartisan or apolitical families, are similar to Butler's and Stokes's. That the Gaullist growth was based on recruitment of the nonimmunized is made further apparent by other data they describe:

> the Gaullists apparently made gains among the formerly uncommitted of all age groups, but above all among older citizens—and in particular, old French women. In 1958, a solid majority of women aged 55 and over had no partisan identification; in 1968, a near majority of these same cohorts was Gaullist, despite the fact that over a fifth of this group was still nonpartisan.[24]

Finally, we can look briefly at the Netherlands, a country where the partisan divisions, in contrast to France, have remained "remarkably constant since the first election under universal manhood suffrage in 1918. Party loyalties have usually been strong and the popular vote very stable."[25] The late 1960s, however, saw seemingly permanent partisan arrangements altered sharply. From 1918 to 1963 the five major parties (Socialist, Liberal, Catholic, and two Protestant parties) controlled about 88 percent of the seats in the Second Chamber. In 1967 this figure dropped to 82 percent, in 1971 to 75 percent. Several new parties came into existence during this period and have managed to capture various numbers of seats in the elections since 1967. It is clear that the new parties have received the bulk of their support from younger voters and, indeed, that younger voters are characterized by a degree of detachment from the traditional parties that could prove significant in the future.

Table 22 shows that fully seventy percent of the youngest age cohort (born in 1947 and later) and over half of the next youngest (born between 1937 and 1946) claimed in 1971 not to identify with any of the five major parties—in striking contrast to the oldest groups. Only 6 percent of the oldest, but a third of the youngest voters supported other parties. Further, of those younger citizens who did identify with a major party, very few were actually members; in general the commitment of younger party supporters was less intense than that of their elders. And Jennings concludes, in a study based on 1970 Dutch data, that "less intense individuals form a natural pool of potential gains for existing parties and initial recruits for new parties. Thus they provide a flexibility, a form of slack in the system, which can be mobilized to meet new conditions."[26]

Table 22   Partisanship by Age Cohorts in the Netherlands, 1971

	Percent supporting		
Cohorts defined by entry into electorate:	5 major parties	other parties	no party
World War I	70%	6%	24%
Interwar	68	14	18
World War II, Occupation	66	13	21
Post-World War II	57	15	28
1960s	48	24	28
Post-1967	30	33	37

Source   These data are from a national survey conducted in 1971 by the Cross-National Project on Political Participation, directed by Sidney Verba and Norman H. Nie.

This discussion is meant to be merely suggestive. But it seems clear that sources of nonimmunization such as generational change, habitual nonvoting, and political circumstances that produce less intense partisan attachments should be considered likely sources of partisan change in party systems that in other respects differ widely from one another.

American Politics in the 1970s

There are clear similarities between the politics of the period preceding the New Deal realignment and present-day party politics. One party was and is clearly in the minority among the population: articles in newspapers and magazines of the mid 1920s speculated about the demise of the Democrats much as similar articles have recently predicted the disappearance of the GOP. Both eras were characterized by a sense that the political choices being offered the public were somehow unsatisfactory. Not entirely coincidentally, political involvement is low, as it was in the twenties. For the earlier period we have only turnout figures, and in the 1920 and 1924 presidential elections less than half of American adults voted. In elections at other levels the turnout was even lower: in the 1922 congressional elections only 36 percent of the national electorate voted.[27] In the mid seventies various measures of political participation and involvement showed a marked drop from a relative high in the 1960s.[28] And turnout in presidential elections, as well as congressional and other elections, appears to be declining steadily.[29]

While immigration is obviously no longer a factor, both turnout and partisan identification are especially low among the young, who are thus possibly the pool from which a mobilizing realignment could draw. The aggregate decline in partisanship over recent years is no longer a matter of conjecture. In 1964, 39 percent of the SRC's national sample said they were "strong" partisans; 23 percent were independents. In 1974, these figures were virtually reversed: 38 percent were independents and only 26 percent were strong partisans.[30] Almost all of this change can be attributed to the very low rates of partisanship of those voters who have entered the electorate since 1964. Cohort analyses indicate that those people who were already of voting age in the 1950s have, for the most part, maintained their former levels of attachment to the parties, while the new voters have entered the electorate with extraordinarily high degrees of nonpartisanship.[31]

The possible outcome of the weakening of partisanship has been a matter of interest and debate. Some more or less traditional realignment scenarios, for example, are offered by David Broder in *The Party's Over*. Rejecting the Kevin Phillips "New Republican Majority" thesis and the Scammon and Wattenberg prediction of a pro-Democratic realignment based on the "social issue," Broder hypothesizes a "coalition for political reform," consisting of blacks, "active and progressive" young people, and educated business and professional people. Should this seem unlikely, he offers a populist coalition of Southerners, blacks, Northern white working class people, and the newly enfranchised young.[32] Phillips's latest book envisions a realignment based on postindustrial categories: the technocrats and knowledge brokers and civil servants will ally with their clients, the poor, against the taxpaying middle classes.[33]

If the plausibility of these alternative futures is to be judged in terms of the mobilization theory, none seems likely to occur. Most of the changes in the party system that we can readily envision are based on realigning issues which are, to a greater or lesser extent, familiar. That is, the economic, regional, and ethnic cleavages which have been important in the past in American politics are the only cleavages, apparently, that we can imagine continuing to be important. Thus a number of the proposed new coalitions would need, in order to succeed, to wrench groups with relatively firm partisan commitments away from their parties. But a new majority, if the realignment is to be based on mobilization rather than conversion, must be created largely from the nonimmunized: in this case, primarily the young. Furthermore, the nonimmunized population must respond more or less uniformly to the redrawing of the lines of conflict which produces and is produced by realignment. The new agenda, which, when offered, will mobilize them into the political system, must have a strong and concrete appeal for the nonimmunized. It is easy, in retrospect, to look at the groups we have identified as being outside the partisan system in the 1920s, like the urban masses, the working class, the immigrants, and many of the young, and to see clearly the interests they shared (particularly after 1929) which made the Democrats so appealing. It is far more difficult to foresee the issues which could mobilize even part of "the largest minority in the world"[34] into full participation in the electoral system.

Partly this is because hindsight is so much easier than prediction, but, in addition, there is the fact that the nonimmunized in the twenties could be thought of in traditional economic and ethnic categories. The homogeneity of the present nonimmunized population is not along these traditional dimensions but primarily along a dimension—age—which has not previously been a long-lasting basis of partisan cleavage. Inglehart argues that the postindustrial age brings with it a new set of (nonmaterialist) value priorities, and those who espouse these values are the young and well-off (precisely those who are the least partisan in the U.S.), and that future political coalitions may in fact be formed on the basis of age and the "postbourgeois mentality" rather than the usual class cleavages.[35] This suggests that if a mobilization-based realignment is to occur, the issues that produce it would more likely be "life-style" issues than economic issues.

At this point, however, it should be noted that a realignment, in the sense that we have come to recognize the phenomenon, is only one of the possible outcomes of the current partisan/electoral drift. Another is an indefinite persistence of the present party cleavages, which is essentially what Sundquist predicts. A third possibility is the continued decay of the party system. Burnham has argued that

> the post-1952 resumption of the march toward electoral disaggregation leads one to suspect the possibility that, in terms of the history of American voting behavior at least, the New Deal might come to be regarded one day as a temporary if massive deviation from a secular trend toward the gradual disappearance of the political party in the United States.[36]

Ladd and Hadley reach similar conclusions in a recent book. The spread of the mass media has usurped the communication and educational functions of the parties and, they ask,

> If substantial segments of the public feel much more confident than they did before in reaching electoral choices without the intervention of parties, and if the role of parties in the communications function has steadily diminished, is it surprising that citizenry loyalties or attachments to political parties have diminished?[37]

Whether or not this dissolution is desirable is open to debate (Ladd and Hadley are positive, Burnham negative). It does raise the question of whether, in fact, "independence" as presently defined (unwillingness to state a party preference when asked to do so on an opinion survey) can be equated with "nonimmunization." It seems entirely possible that independence has many of the psychological attributes of party identification—that people who so characterize themselves (especially those who are young and well-educated) do so not out of a negative feeling toward the parties but out of a positive commitment to nonpartisanship. This argument is supported indirectly by Beck, who sets age 30 as a limit above which people are no longer mobilizable.[38] This seems rather arbitrary, but it serves to point up the fact that any habitual behavior—even if it is *not* voting or *not* supporting a party—becomes, with time, difficult to change. And if the parties' role in American politics continues to weaken, there is reason to believe that the currently "nonimmunized" may become, in effect, "immunized" against traditional party loyalties.

Notes

Preface

1 Everett C. Ladd, Jr., Charles Hadley, and Lauriston King, "A New Political Realignment," and James L. Sundquist, "The Myth of New Majorities," in Edward C. Dreyer and Walter Rosenbaum, eds., *Political Opinion and Behavior*, 2d ed. (Belmont, Calif.: Wadsworth, 1976).

2 James L. Sundquist, *Dynamics of the Party System* (Washington, D.C.: Brookings Institution, 1973).

3 Samuel Lubell, *The Future of American Politics* (New York: Harper & Row, 1951); Angus Campbell, et al., *The American Voter* (New York: John Wiley, 1960), pp. 153–56.

Chapter One

1 Carl Degler, "American Political Parties and the Rise of the City: An Interpretation," *Journal of American History* 51 (June 1964): 41–59.

2 For the notion that there are a finite number of social cleavages to be represented and that they have been taken care of by the present European party systems,

135

see S. M. Lipset and Stein Rokkan, *Party Systems and Voter Alignments* (New York: Free Press, 1967), pp. 50–56.

3   V. O. Key, "A Theory of Critical Elections," *Journal of Politics* 17 (February 1955): 4.

4   Walter Dean Burnham, *Critical Elections and the Mainsprings of American Politics* (New York: W. W. Norton, 1970).

5   Sundquist, *Dynamics*, p. 3.

6   Duncan MacRae, Jr., and James A. Meldrum, "Critical Elections in Illinois: 1888–1958," *American Political Science Review* 54 (September 1960): 669–83.

7   Jerome M. Clubb and Howard W. Allen, "The Cities and the Election of 1928: Partisan Realignment?" in *Electoral Change and Stability in American Political History*, ed. Jerome M. Clubb and Howard W. Allen (New York: Free Press, 1971), pp. 236–54.

8   John L. Shover, "Was 1928 a Critical Election in California?" in Clubb and Allen, *Electoral Change and Stability*, pp. 215–34. See also John L. Shover, "The Emergence of a Two-Party System in Republican Philadelphia, 1924–1936," *Journal of Interdisciplinary History* 60 (1974): 1000–1002.

9   It should be noted that the term "critical election *theory*" is used somewhat loosely. In a recent article, Lichtman states that "Political scientists have not carefully distinguished between descriptive and defining features of critical elections" (see Allan J. Lichtman, "Critical Election Theory and the Reality of American Presidential Politics, 1916–1940," *American Historical Review* 81 [April 1976]: 342). Lichtman further argues that "the theory includes no objective procedures for translating a set of statistical associations between elections into statements expressing the proper classification of each election." The concept of "realignment" is broader and has fewer claims to theoretical precision. The notion that there have been several distinct American "party systems," brought into being by realignments in the coalitional bases of the parties, is widely accepted. As will become obvious, the use of the "critical election" perspective has tended to obscure the mechanisms by which realignments take place; hence the "theory" of critical elections will not be used in this work.

10   Sundquist, *Dynamics*, p. 29; Burnham, *Critical Elections*, p. 10.

11   Key, "Theory of Critical Elections," pp. 5,7.

12   Burnham, *Critical Elections*, p. 6.

13   Ibid., p. 67.

14   Campbell, et al., *The American Voter*, p. 137.

15   M. Kent Jennings and Richard Niemi, "The Transmission of Political Values from Parent to Child," *American Political Science Review* 62 (March 1968): 168–84.

16   Campbell, et al., *The American Voter*, p. 149.

17   *Dynamics*, p. 6.

18   Ibid., p. 7.

19 Campbell, et al., *The American Voter*, p. 149.
20 Ibid, p. 151.
21 Philip E. Converse, "Public Opinion and Voting Behavior," in *Handbook of Political Science*, vol. 1, ed. Nelson W. Polsby and Fred I. Greenstein (Reading, Mass.: Addison-Wesley, 1975), p. 140.
22 Key, "Theory of Critical Elections"; Shover, "Was 1928 a Critical Election"; Degler, "American Political Parties and the Rise of the City"; Clubb and Allen, "The Cities and the Election of 1928"; W. Phillips Shively, "A Reinterpretation of the New Deal Realignment," *Public Opinion Quarterly* 35 (Winter 1971–72): 620–24; Lichtman, "Critical Election Theory."
23 "The Cities and the Election of 1928," p. 238.
24 V. O. Key, "Secular Realignment and the Party System," *Journal of Politics* 21 (May 1959): 198–210.
25 Lubell, *Future*, pp. 28–33.
26 Degler, "The Rise of the City," pp. 135–37.
27 David Burner, *The Politics of Provincialism: The Democratic Party in Transition, 1918–1932* (New York: Alfred A. Knopf, 1968), p. 229.
28 Lubell, *Future*, p. 29.
29 V. O. Key, *The Responsible Electorate* (New York: Random House, Vintage Books, 1966), p. 53.
30 For example, Gerald M. Pomper, "From Confusion to Clarity: Issues and American Voters, 1956–1968," *American Political Science Review* 66 (June, 1972): 415–28.
31 David Butler and Donald Stokes (*Political Change in Britain* [New York: St. Martin's Press, 1969], pp. 283–86) have shown that even short-term change, such as the Conservative reversal between 1959 and 1963, can sometimes be accounted for mostly by new voters rather than switchers.
32 "Social Determinism and Rationality as Bases of Party Identification," *American Political Science Review* 63 (March, 1969): 5–25.
33 "From Confusion to Clarity," p. 467.
34 Charles Sellers, "The Equilibrium Cycle in Two-Party Politics," *Public Opinion Quarterly* 29 (Spring, 1965): 26.
35 See, for example, Walter Dean Burnham, "The Changing Shape of the American Political Universe," *American Political Science Review* 59 (March 1965): 7–28.
36 Chilton Williamson, *American Suffrage from Property to Democracy, 1760–1870* (Princeton, N.J.: Princeton University Press, 1960). See also Stanley Kelley, Jr., Richard Ayres, and William G. Bowen, "Registration and Voting: Putting First Things First," *American Political Science Review* 61 (June 1967): 359–77; Jae-On Kim, John R. Petrocik, and Stephen N. Enokson, "Voter Turnout among the American States: Systemic and Individual Components," *American Political Science Review* 69 (March 1975): 107–30.

37   The impact of European immigrants on the politics of western Can-
     ada in the first half of the twentieth century is suggested by S. M.
     Lipset in *Agrarian Socialism* (New York: Doubleday, 1968), chap. 8.

38   Lubell, *Future*; Degler, "American Political Parties and The Rise of
     the City"; Burner, *Politics of Provincialism*, chap. 8.

39   *The Winning of the Midwest: Social and Political Conflict, 1888–
     1896* (Chicago: University of Chicago Press, 1971), pp. 58–88, 301.

40   Jennings and Niemi, "Transmission."

41   See, for example, Jennings and Niemi, "Transmission," pp. 171–72;
     Eleanor E. Maccoby, Richard E. Matthews, and Anton S. Morton,
     "Youth and Political Change," *Public Opinion Quarterly* 18 (Spring
     1954): 23–29; Robert E. Lane, "Fathers and Sons: Foundations of
     Political Belief," *American Sociological Review* 24 (August 1959):
     502–11; Richard W. Dodge and Eugene S. Uyeki, "Political Affilia-
     tion and Imagery across Two Related Generations," *Midwest Jour-
     nal of Politics* 6 (1962): 266–76.

42   Benjamin I. Page and Raymond Wolfinger, "Party Identification," in
     Readings in American Political Behavior, ed. Raymond Wolfinger
     (Englewood Cliffs, N.J.: Prentice-Hall, 1970), p. 296.

43   M. Kent Jennings and Richard G. Niemi, "Continuity and Change
     in Political Orientations: A Longitudinal Study of Generations,"
     American Political Science Review 69 (December 1975): 1327–28.

44   Norval Glenn, "Class and Party Support in the United States: Re-
     cent and Emerging Trends," *Public Opinion Quarterly* 37 (Spring
     1973): 1–20.

45   Paul Abramson, "Generational Change and the Decline of Party
     Identification in America: 1952–1974," *American Political Science
     Review* 70 (June 1976): 101; Butler and Stokes, *Political Change
     in Britain*, pp. 110–18.

46   Butler and Stokes, *Political Change in Britain*, p. 36.

47   Sundquist, *Dynamics*, p. 7.

48   E. E. Schattschneider, *The Semi-Sovereign People* (New York:
     Holt, Rinehart, & Winston, 1960), p. 112.

49   Campbell, et al., *The American Voter*, pp. 92–93; Burnham, "Chang-
     ing Shape."

50   Schattschneider, *The Semi-Sovereign People*, p. 98.

51   Key, "A Theory of Critical Elections," p. 4.

52   Burnham, *Critical Elections*, pp. 6–8.

53   Charles E. Merriam and Harold F. Gosnell, *Non-Voting* (Chicago:
     University of Chicago Press, 1924), pp. 251–52.

54   Bernard P. Berelson, Paul F. Lazarsfeld, and William N. McPhee,
     Voting (Chicago: University of Chicago Press, 1954), p. 32.

55   The analysis in *The American Voter* (chap. 5) is similar to that in
     Voting but even less penetrating: low turnout is explained by lack
     of political involvement, but reasons for this noninvolvement are not
     advanced.

56 Schattschneider, *The Semi-Sovereign People*, p. 105. In contrast, Przeworski begins with the assumption that the "preferences" and "interests" (no distinction is made between the two) of the newly mobilized are different from those of the voting population they join but concludes, in effect, that they are not. Adam Przeworski, "Institutionalization of Voting Patterns, or Is Mobilization the Source of Decay?" *American Political Science Review* 69 (March 1975): 49–67.

Chapter Two

1 *Critical Elections*, pp. 7–8.
2 "The Changing Shape of the American Political Universe," *American Political Science Review* 59 (March 1965): 1–28. This is not a criticism of Burnham. If one argues that changes in the size of the electorate can be, at different times, both cause and result of partisan change, there is no reason that both patterns have to be considered by everyone interested in realignments or critical elections.
3 For example, Lubell, *Future*, chap. 3; Degler, "American Political Parties and the Rise of the City," pp. 134–41.
4 U.S. Bureau of the Census, *Statistical Abstract of the United States: 1975* (Washington, D.C.: Government Printing Office, 1975), p. 99.
5 Philip E. Converse, "Of Time and Partisan Stability," *Comparative Political Studies* 2 (July 1969): 139–71.
6 Ibid., p. 170.
7 Joel Goldstein, "The Effects of the Adoption of Woman Suffrage: Sex Differences in Voting—Illinois 1914–1921" (Ph.D. thesis, University of Chicago, 1973), p. 135.
8 That is, on the basis of issues alone the party system is not speaking to everyone. If the parties perform the function of crystallizing group loyalties and routinizing political participation, however, "issue irrelevance" may not lead people to withdraw from the system.
9 Burnham, *Critical Elections*, pp. 19–20.
10 Ibid., p. 17; Wilfred E. Binkley, *American Political Parties: Their Natural History*, 4th ed. (New York: Alfred A. Knopf, 1971), p. 305.
11 The sources for the total number of votes cast in presidential elections were Walter Dean Burnham, *Presidential Ballots 1836–1892* (Baltimore: Johns Hopkins Press, 1955) and Congressional Quarterly, *Presidential Elections since 1789* (Washington, D.C.: Congressional Quarterly, 1975).

The percentage increase from one election year to the next was averaged over the four-year period so that, for example, the 11 percent increase in the total votes cast between 1956 and 1960 became a 2.75 percent yearly increase.

The determination of the "potential electorate" presents far greater problems, and this figure is based on a rather crude representation of the change in size of the electorate. In fact, what is measured here is population increase, not growth in the potential electorate per se. The figures on which population change is calculated are the total male population before 1920 and the total population in 1920 and afterwards. The rate of change of the total population, of course, is not identical to the rate of change of the potential electorate (adult males before 1920; adults of both sexes from then on). Because the age structure has changed over the years to produce a current population substantially older than that of the early nineteenth century, the numbers on which this figure is based are misleading in the following way: the growth of the electorate is overstated slightly in the mid nineteenth century and understated slightly by the mid twentieth century. However, the secular trends in the relationship between potential and actual electorate expansion should not be affected by the crudeness of our population measure.

The percentage change in population from census to census was averaged over the ten-year period to obtain an estimate of yearly change.

To obtain the ratio presented in fig. 1, the average "yearly change" in vote was divided by the estimated yearly change in population for each election year. Thus for the year 1880, the figure .77 is arrived at by dividing 2.4 percent (the yearly vote increase which cumulates to a 9.6 percent increase between 1876 and 1880) by 3.09 percent (one tenth of the 30.9 percent increase in the population between 1870 and 1880). In the case of four-year periods that fall into two decades, the denominator is the average rate of change for the two decades. For the years 1912 and 1916, the rate of population change was based on the growth of the male population only.

12 Burnham, "Changing Shape," p. 24.
13 Burner, *Politics of Provincialism*, pp. 228–29; Degler, "American Political Parties and the Rise of the City," pp. 137–41.
14 Sundquist, *Dynamics*, p. 200.
15 Ibid., chap. 10; Converse, "Public Opinion and Voting Behavior," p. 141.
16 The difference between total votes and Republican votes includes, of course, "other" votes, which are not especially significant except for the Progressive vote in 1924.
17 These calculations are based on the figures presented in Degler, "American Political Parties and the Rise of the City," pp. 139–40.
18 Angus Campbell, "Surge and Decline: A Study in Electoral Change," in *Elections and the Political Order*, ed. Angus Campbell, et al., (New York: John Wiley, 1966), p. 49.

19 Sundquist, *Dynamics*, p. 204.
20 Ibid., pp. 204–8; see Converse, "Public Opinion and Voting Behavior," p. 141.

Chapter Three

1 Walter Lippmann, "The Causes of Political Indifference Today," in *Men of Destiny* (New York: Macmillan, 1927), pp. 18–34; A. M. Schlesinger and E. M. Erickson, "The Vanishing Voter," *New Republic*, October 15, 1924.
2 Burnham, "Changing Shape," pp. 4–5.
3 Walter Dean Burnham, "Theory and Voting Research: Some Reflections on Converse's 'Change in the American Electorate,'" *American Political Science Review* 68 (September 1974): 1013.
4 Merriam and Gosnell, *Non-Voting*, p. 26.
5 Goldstein, "The Effects of the Adoption of Woman Suffrage," p. 135.
6 Lubell, *Future*, p. 28.
7 The extent to which this tendency could be reversed by hard-working local party machines is documented and discussed by Merriam and Gosnell, *Non-Voting*, chap. 8.
8 David Prindle, "Mobilization and Realignment in Pittsburgh, 1920–1940" (unpublished manuscript, Massachusetts Institute of Technology, 1975).
9 Merriam and Gosnell, *Non-Voting*, p. 28.
10 Sources for these figures are the *Chicago Daily News Almanac, 1926*, pp. 809, 814 for registration and estimated population, and *Census Data of the City of Chicago, 1930*, for percent foreign-born and data on rents.
11 Sundquist, *Dynamics*, p. 281.
12 Paul Allen Beck, "A Socialization Theory of Partisan Realignment," in *New Views of Children and Politics*, ed. Richard Niemi (San Francisco: Jossey-Bass, 1974).
13 Cambell, et al., *The American Voter*, p. 162; Norman H. Nie, Sidney Verba, and John R. Petrocik, *The Changing American Voter* (Cambridge: Harvard University Press, 1976), chap. 4.
14 Ronald Inglehart and Avram Hochstein, "Alignment and Dealignment of the Electorate in France and the United States," *Comparative Political Studies* 5 (October 1972): 343–72.
15 Ibid., p. 354.
16 Nie, Verba, and Petrocik, *The Changing American Voter*, chap. 4.
17 Though "retrospective" survey data—i.e., data on the respondents' past political behavior—will be used in the next chapter to characterize the electorate in the twenties and thirties, it will be shown that the measurement of the proportion independent in a given year by this method is less than perfect.

18   Merriam and Gosnell, *Non-Voting*, p. 29.

19   Ben Arnesen, "Non-Voting in a Typical Ohio Community," *American Political Science Review* 19 (November, 1925): 816–26. Arnesen notes that his work was inspired by Charles Merriam.

20   Burnham, *Critical Elections*, p. 10. It is interesting to note that this kind of "stress" model of political change is widely used to explain revolutionary movements. See, for example, Chalmers Johnson, *Revolutionary Change* (Boston: Little, Brown, 1966).

21   Burnham, *Critical Elections*, pp. 180–81.

22   Schattschneider, *The Semi-Sovereign People*, p. 75.

23   Anthony Downs, *An Economic Theory of Democracy* (New York: Harper & Row, 1957), p. 39.

24   Richard Brody and Benjamin I. Page, "Indifference, Alienation and Rational Decisions: The Effects of Candidate Evaluations on Turnout and the Vote," *Public Choice* 15 (Summer 1973): 1–17.

25   Paul Douglas, "The Prospects for a New Political Alignment," *American Political Science Review* 25 (November 1931): 906–7.

26   I. B. Taeuber and C. Taeuber, *People of the U.S.* (Washington, D.C.: Bureau of the Census, 1971), p. 67.

27   Ibid., p. 101.

28   Ibid., pp. 119 and 99. This pattern was particularly marked among some of the immigrant groups. The Dillingham Commission in 1911 found that 81.5 percent of Polish immigrants had been farmers or farm laborers; about two-thirds were unskilled laborers in the United States (Edward R. Kantowicz, *Polish-American Politics in Chicago, 1888–1940* [Chicago: University of Chicago Press, 1975], p. 28).

29   Such generalizations ignore, of course, the particular situations in individual cities. The role of the local party organizations in at least one city, Chicago, will be touched upon in a later chapter.

30   Degler, "American Political Parties and the Rise of the City," pp. 127–28.

31   Binkley, *American Political Parties*, pp. 367–68.

32   Burner, *Politics of Provincialism*, p. 64.

33   Everett Carll Ladd, Jr., *American Political Parties* (New York: W. W. Norton, 1970), p. 163.

34   Paul Douglas, "The Prospects for a New Political Alignment," pp. 912–13.

Chapter Four

1   For an interpretation of the realignment that leans heavily on this poll's 1936 debacle, see Shively, "A Reinterpretation."

2   The 1962 and 1966 data sets were not used, since questions on past party identification were not asked in those years.

3   People who say they are supporters of a party and have never changed are not probed to see if they were ever independent. Some "always Democrats" or "always Republicans" have considered themselves independent when they first entered the electorate. This point will be returned to later.

4   Age distributions are from the U.S. census. For years between censuses, the population in each age group was interpolated; this is the method used by the Census Bureau for such estimations until the late 1940s. See U.S. Department of Commerce, Bureau of the Census, *Nineteenth Census of the United States, 1970*, vol. 1, part 1, table 51.

5   Cf. Butler and Stokes, *Political Change*, pp. 263–74; David Segal, et al., "Mortality and Political Partisanship: A Test of the Butler-Stokes Hypothesis," *Comparative Politics* 5 (July 1973): 601–10.

6   The Gallup differences are in the opposite direction from the SRC data, i.e., they report fewer Democrats. Mueller suggests that at least until 1952 and possibly later Gallup's sample consistently underrepresented lower class persons and therefore Democrats (John E. Mueller, *War, Presidents and Public Opinion* [New York: John Wiley & Sons, 1973]).

7   Sundquist, *Dynamics*, ch. 17.

8   Butler and Stokes, *Political Change*, p. 59. See also Karl Mannheim, "The Problem of Generations," in *Essays on the Sociology of Knowledge*, ed. Paul Kecskemeti (London: Routledge & Kegan Paul, 1947); Converse, "Time and Partisan Stability"; Ronald Inglehart, "The Silent Revolution in Europe: Intergenerational Change in Post-Industrial Societies," *American Political Science Review* 65 (December 1971): 991–1017.

9   Butler and Stokes, after describing a somewhat similar reconstruction of the party affiliation of various age cohorts, conclude: "The full array can indeed be seen as underlining the importance that the physical turnover of the electorate has for the broadest and most lasting electoral changes. Some of the change recorded in these estimates reflects transient shifts of support. . . . But our estimates here show most of all the role which the replenishment of the electorate has played in the great changes of alignment that have characterized British politics in this century" (*Political Change*, p. 274).

10   These figures and subsequent data on respondents' first vote are based on answers to questions asked, unfortunately, only in the 1952 election study: "Do you remember who you voted for the first time you voted for president?" "Do you remember what year that was?" The data are similar but not identical to those presented by Campbell, et al., *The American Voter*, p. 155. They differ in that the "first voters 28 or under" category here includes some of their "delayed first voters." This distinction makes the biggest difference in 1928, which will be more understandable a bit later in this chapter.

11   Burnham, "Changing Shape," p. 23.

12   A high Republican defection rate, as well as a highly Democratic independent vote, in the 1932 election may have accounted for much of Roosevelt's margin of victory. In the 1936 election 20 percent of FDR's total vote, according to a 1937 Gallup poll, came from Republicans and independents.

Chapter Five

1   This is a recalculation from the figures in table 7-1 in Campbell, et al., *The American Voter.*

2   Converse, "Public Opinion and Voting Behavior"; Beck, "Socialization Theory of Realignment."

3   In both cases the figures are based on a threefold classification of partisanship: Democrat, independent, and Republican. See Jennings and Niemi, "Transmission."

4   Converse, "Public Opinion and Voting Behavior."

5   Taeuber and Taeuber, *People of the U.S.,* p. 445.

6   Lubell, *Future,* p. 30.

7   Cf. Campbell, et al., *The American Voter,* p. 155.

8   Actually the following analysis will be based on recall of the respondents' father's partisanship only. In most cases the mother's partisanship agreed with that of the father or was not recalled by the respondent; in this period one can argue that paternal partisan cues were the more significant.

9   Richard G. Niemi, *How Family Members Perceive Each Other* (New Haven and London: Yale University Press, 1974), pp. 51–62.

10   Ibid., p. 59.

Chapter Six

1   Lubell, *Future,* p. 29.

2   John M. Allswang, *A House for All Peoples* (Lexington: University Press of Kentucky, 1971), p. 272.

3   Charles Merriam, *Chicago: A More Intimate View of Urban Politics* (New York: Macmillan, 1929), p. 5.

4   Philip E. Converse, "The Problems of Party Distances in Models of Voting Change," in *The Electoral Process,* ed. M. Kent Jennings and Harmon Zeigler (Englewood Cliffs, N.J.: Prentice-Hall, 1966).

5   Ibid., p. 178.

6   U.S. Department of Commerce, Bureau of the Census, *Religious Bodies, 1936* (Washington, D.C.: Government Printing Office, 1936), 1:480–82.

7   Mike Royko, *Boss: Richard J. Daley of Chicago* (New York: Dutton, 1972), pp. 24–25.

8   John P. Gavit, *Americans by Choice* (New York: Harper Bros., 1922), pp. 236–38.

9   Allswang, *House*, p. 22.

10   Merriam, *Chicago*, p. 99.

11   Ibid., p. 96.

12   Allswang, *House*, p. 119.

13   Merriam, *Chicago*, p. 137.

14   Allswang, *House*, p. 34.

15   Ibid., chaps. 2 and 3.

16   Ibid., p. 35.

17   Ibid., p. 42.

18   Harold F. Gosnell, *Machine Politics: Chicago Model* (Chicago: University of Chicago Press, 1937), p. 32. See also Merriam, *Chicago*, p. 152.

19   Key, "Theory of Critical Elections."

20   In chap. 2 both the expansion of the potential electorate and the expansion of the actual electorate were discussed as playing a part in realignments. Because the ward boundaries change, it is impossible in this portion of the analysis to consider growth in the potential electorate in a given political unit; so we can only consider the growth of the actual electorate, i.e., the change in the turnout.

21   Ernest W. Burgess and Charles Newcomb, *Census Data of the City of Chicago, 1920* (Chicago: University of Chicago Press, 1933).

22   The 1924 population of wards is an estimation as of July 1, 1925, by the municipal reference librarian, as published in the *Chicago Daily News Almanac* (1926), p. 809. The 1930 populations of the wards drawn in 1921 are from U.S. Bureau of the Census, *Fifteenth Census of the United States: 1930. Population*, 1. The wards were redrawn in 1931, and their estimated populations as of 1930 were found in a mimeographed publication of the Chicago Municipal Reference Library, "Population data as of July 1st, 1936 for the City of Chicago by Wards." The 1940 population figures (for the wards drawn in 1931) are from U.S. Bureau of the Census, *Sixteenth Census of the United States: 1940*, vol. 11, part 2. The same source was used for the number of people over 21, number of foreign-born, and number of blacks in each ward. Estimates of ward populations for years when census data were not available were arrived at by interpolation. Votes by wards for 1924 and 1928 are from the *Chicago Daily News Almanac* of 1925 and 1929, respectively. The same source (1925:772) was used for the number of people registered in each ward. Voting data for 1932 and 1936 are from the *Public Service Leader*, November 1932 and November 1936. For 1940 vote returns by wards were found in the *Chicago Tribune*.

23 Compare this with Gosnell, *Machine Politics*, pp. 120–22.
24 Allswang (*House*, p. 155) points out that one of the farsighted policies adopted by Cermak during his rise to power in the 1920s was the abandonment of the traditionally anti-Negro tenor of Democratic campaigns, so that the ground was prepared for organization of the 2d ward during the thirties.
25 It should be remembered that these are actually groups of wards, totalling eleven in the twenties and nine after 1931.
26 All of the white ethnic groups Allswang studied gave a majority of their three-party presidential vote to Coolidge; six also produced a Republican majority for senator and governor (*House*, p. 42).
27 Merriam and Gosnell, *Non-Voting*, pp. 39–41.
28 MacRae and Meldrum, "Critical Elections in Illinois," p. 670.
29 Allswang, *House*, p. 62.
30 Shover, "Was 1928 a Critical Election?"
31 Burner, *Politics of Provincialism*, p. 230.
32 Because the population data is for areas larger than precincts, the potential electorate in a precinct or group of precincts cannot be estimated.
33 Allswang, *House*, p. 224.
34 For example, Bernard R. Berelson, Paul F. Lazarsfeld, and William N. McPhee, *Voting* (Chicago: University of Chicago Press, 1954), chap. 6.
35 Taeuber and Taeuber, *People of the U.S.*, p. 506.

Conclusion

1 William McPhee and Jack Ferguson, "Political Immunization," in William McPhee and Nathan Glazer, *Public Opinion and Congressional Elections* (New York: Free Press, 1966), pp. 175–76.
2 S. M. Lipset, *Political Man* (Garden City, N.Y.: Doubleday, 1960), pp. 149–52; Karl O'Lessker, "Who Voted for Hitler? A New Look at the Class Basis of Naziism," *American Journal of Sociology* 74 (July 1968): 66–67.
3 Walter Dean Burnham, "Political Immunization and Political Confessionalism," *Journal of Interdisciplinary History* 13 (Winter 1972–73): 1–30.
4 Ibid., p. 29.
5 Lester W. Milbrath, *Political Participation* (Chicago: Rand McNally, 1965), p. 146.
6 Sundquist, *Dynamics*, p. 65.
7 Ibid., p. 72.
8 Jensen, *Winning of the Midwest*, chap. 3; Paul Kleppner, *The Cross of Culture: A Social Analysis of Midwestern Politics 1850–1900* (New York: Free Press, 1970), chap. 2.

9 Ronald P. Formisano, *The Birth of Mass Political Parties: Michigan, 1827–1861* (Princeton, N.J.: Princeton University Press, 1971), p. 322.

10 John R. Petrocik, "Changing Party Coalitions and the Attitudinal Basis of Realignment: 1952–1972" (Ph.D. thesis, University of Chicago, 1975), pp. 70–80.

11 Burnham, "Changing Shape," p. 11.

12 Sundquist, *Dynamics*, pp. 147–51; Burnham, *Critical Elections*, pp. 39–41.

13 Degler, "American Political Parties and The Rise of the City," pp. 43–44.

14 Ibid., p. 43.

15 Samuel P. Hays, *The Response to Industrialism 1885–1914* (Chicago: University of Chicago Press, 1957), p. 47.

16 See, for example, Jensen, *Winning of the Midwest*; Samuel Mc-Seveney, *The Politics of Depression: Political Behavior in the Northeast, 1893–1896* (New York: Oxford University Press, 1972).

17 For a nice comparative analysis of party identification in Norway and the United States, see Angus Campbell and Henry Valen, "Party Identification in Norway and the United States," *Public Opinion Quarterly* 25 (Fall 1961): 505–25. See also Philip Converse and George Dupeux, "Politicization of the Electorate in France and the U.S.," *Public Opinion Quarterly* 26 (Spring 1962): 1–23; Richard Rose and Derek Urwin, "Social Cohesion, Political Parties and Regimes," *Comparative Political Studies* 2 (April 1969): 1–67.

18 Butler and Stokes, *Political Change*, p. 258.

19 Ibid., p. 284.

20 Ibid., pp. 288–89.

21 Giacomo Sani, "Secular Trends and Party Realignments in Italy: The 1975 Election," paper presented at the American Political Science Association Meetings, San Francisco, September 1975.

22 Richard Rose and Derek Urwin, "Persistence and Change in Western Party Systems since 1945," *Political Studies* 18 (Summer 1970): 311.

23 Inglehart and Hochstein, "Alignment and Dealignment," p. 357.

24 Ibid., p. 359.

25 Arend Lijphart, *The Politics of Accommodation: Pluralism and Democracy in the Netherlands* (Berkeley: University of California Press, 1968, p. 5).

26 M. Kent Jennings, "Partisan Commitment and Electoral Behavior in the Netherlands," (mimeographed, 1972), p. 29.

27 Walter Dean Burnham, "The United States: The Politics of Heterogeneity," in *Electoral Behavior: A Comparative Handbook*, ed. Richard Rose (New York: Free Press, 1974), p. 677.

28 Nie, Verba, and Petrocik, *The Changing American Voter*, pp. 273–75.

29   Burnham, "Politics of Heterogeneity."
30   Nie, Verba, and Petrocik, *The Changing American Voter*, p. 49.
31   Ibid., pp. 59–66; Paul Abramson, "Generational Change and the Decline of Party Identification in America: 1952–1974," *American Political Science Review* 70 (June 1976): 469–78; Norval D. Glenn, "Sources of the Shift to Political Independence: Some Evidence from Cohort Analysis," *Social Science Quarterly* 53 (Fall 1972): 494–519.
32   David S. Broder, *The Party's Over: The Failure of Politics in America* (New York: Harper & Row, 1971), pp. 204–8.
33   Kevin Phillips, *Mediacracy* (New York: Doubleday, 1975).
34   Schattschneider, *Semi-Sovereign People*, p. 108.
35   Inglehart, "Silent Revolution."
36   Burnham, *Critical Elections*, pp. 132–33.
37   Everett C. Ladd, Jr., and Charles D. Hadley, *Transformations of the American Party System* (New York: W. W. Norton, 1975), p. 337.
38   Beck, "Socialization Theory of Realignment," p. 16.

Selected Bibliography

Abramson, Paul. "Generational Change and the Decline of Party Identification in America: 1952–1974." *American Political Science Review* 70 (June 1976): 469–78.

————. "Generational Change in American Electoral Behavior." *American Political Science Review* 68 (1974): 93–104.

Allswang, John M. *A House for All Peoples.* Lexington: University Press of Kentucky, 1971.

Arnesen, Ben. "Non-voting in a Typical Ohio Community." *American Political Science Review* 19 (1925): 816–26.

Beck, Paul Allen. "A Socialization Theory of Partisan Realignment." In *Controversies in American Voting Behavior*, edited by Richard Niemi and Herbert Weisberg, pp. 396–411. San Francisco: W. H. Freeman, 1976.

Berelson, Bernard R.; Lazarfeld, Paul F.; and McPhee, William N. *Voting.* Chicago: University of Chicago Press, 1954.

Bernstein, Irving. *The Lean Years: A History of the American Worker 1920–1933*. Boston: Houghton Mifflin, 1960.

Binkley, Wilfred E. *American Political Parties: Their Natural History*. 4th ed. New York: Alfred A. Knopf, 1971.

Boyd, Richard W. "Popular Control of Public Policy: A Normal Vote Analysis of the 1968 Election." *American Political Science Review* 66 (June 1972): 429–49.

Broder, David S. *The Party's Over: The Failure of Politics in America*. New York: Harper & Row, 1971.

Brody, Richard, and Page, Benjamin I. "Indifference, Alienation and Rational Decisions: The Effects of Candidate Evaluations on Turnout and the Vote." *Public Choice* 15 (Summer 1973): 1–17.

Burgess, Ernest W., and Newcomb, Charles. *Census Data of the City of Chicago, 1920*. Chicago: University of Chicago, 1931.

————. *Census Data of the City of Chicago, 1930*. Chicago: University of Chicago Press, 1933.

Burner, David. *The Politics of Provincialism: The Democratic Party in Transition, 1918–1932*. New York: Alfred A. Knopf, 1968.

Burnham, Walter Dean. "The Changing Shape of the American Political Universe." *American Political Science Review* 59 (March 1965): 7–28.

————. *Critical Elections and the Mainsprings of American Politics*. New York: W. W. Norton, 1970.

————. "Political Immunization and Political Confessionalism." *Journal of Interdisciplinary History* 3 (1972–73): 1–30.

————. *Presidential Ballots 1836–1892*. Baltimore: Johns Hopkins Press, 1955.

————. "Theory and Voting Research: Some Reflections on Converse's 'Change in the American Electorate.'" *American Political Science Review* 68 (September 1974): 1002–22.

Butler, David, and Stokes, Donald. *Political Change in Britain*. New York: St. Martin's Press, 1969.

Cameron, David R. "Stability and Change in Patterns of French Partisanship." *Public Opinion Quarterly* 36 (1972–73): 19–32.

Campbell, Angus; Converse, P.; Miller, W.; and Stokes, D. *The American Voter*. New York: John Wiley, 1960.

———. *Elections and the Political Order*. New York: John Wiley, 1966.

Campbell, Angus, and Valen, Henry. "Party Identification in Norway and the United States." *Public Opinion Quarterly* 25 (1961): 505–25.

Chambers, William Nisbet, and Burnham, Walter Dean. *The American Party Systems*. New York: Oxford University Press, 1967.

Chicago Daily News Almanac and Yearbook (1921–37).

Clubb, Jerome M., and Allen, Howard W. "The Cities and the Election of 1928: Partisan Realignment?" *Electoral Change and Stability in American Political History*, edited by Jerome M. Clubb and Howard W. Allen, pp. 236–54. New York: Free Press, 1971.

Congressional Quarterly. "Presidential Elections since 1789." Washington, D.C.: Congressional Quarterly, 1975.

Converse, Philip E. "The Problems of Party Distances in Models of Voting Change." In *The Electoral Process*, edited by M. Kent Jennings and Harmon Zeigler, pp. 175–207. Englewood Cliffs, N.J.: Prentice-Hall, 1966.

———. "Public Opinion and Voting Behavior." In *Handbook of Political Science*, vol. 4, edited by Fred I. Greenstein and Nelson W. Polsby, pp. 75–169. Reading, Mass.: Addison Wesley, 1975.

———. "Of Time and Partisan Stability." *Comparative Political Studies* 2 (July 1969): 139–71.

Converse, Philip E., and Dupeux, G. "Politicization of the Electorate in France and the U.S." *Public Opinion Quarterly* 26 (Spring 1962): 1–23.

Cutler, Neil. "Generation, Maturation and Party Affiliation." *Public Opinion Quarterly* 33 (Winter 1969–70): 589–91.

Degler, Carl. "American Political Parties and the Rise of the City: An Interpretation." *Journal of American History* 51 (June 1964): 41–59.

Douglas, Paul. "The Prospects for a New Political Alignment." *American Political Science Review* 25 (November 1931): 906–7.

Downs, Anthony. *An Economic Theory of Democracy*. New York: Harper & Row, 1957.

Dreyer, Edward C., and Rosenbaum, Walter. *Political Opinion and Behavior*. 3d ed. Belmont, Calif.: Wadsworth, 1976.

Eldersveld, Samuel. "The Influence of Metropolitan Party Pluralities in Presidential Elections since 1920." *American Political Science Review* 43 (December 1949): 1189–1226.

Glenn, Norval C. "Class and Party Support in the United States: Recent and Emerging Trends." *Public Opinion Quarterly* 37 (Spring 1973): 1–20.

————. "Sources of the Shift to Political Independence: Some Evidence from a Cohort Analysis." *Social Science Quarterly* 53 (Fall 1972): 494–519.

Goldberg, Arthur S. "Social Determinism and Rationality as Bases of Party Identification." *American Political Science Review* 63 (March 1969): 5–25.

Goldstein, Joel H. "The Effects of the Adoption of Woman Suffrage: Sex Differences in Voting Behavior: Illinois 1914–1921." Ph.D. thesis, University of Chicago, 1973.

Gosnell, H. F. *Machine Politics, Chicago Model*. Chicago: University of Chicago Press, 1937.

Hays, Samuel P. *The Response to Industrialism 1885–1914*. Chicago: University of Chicago Press, 1957.

————. "The Social Analysis of American Political History 1880–1920." *Political Science Quarterly* 80 (September 1965): 373–94.

Hicks, John D. *Republican Ascendancy 1921–1933*. New York: Harper & Row, 1960.

Hyman, Herbert H. *Political Socialization*. Glencoe: Free Press, 1959.

Inglehart, Ronald. "The Silent Revolution in Europe: Intergenerational Change in Post-Industrial Societies." *American Political Science Review* 65 (1971): 991–1017.

Inglehart, Ronald, and Hochstein, Avram. "Alignment and Dealignment of the Electorate in France and the United States." *Comparative Political Studies* 5 (October 1972): 343–72.

Jahnige, Thomas P. "Critical Elections and Social Change." *Polity* 3 (Summer 1971): 466–500.

Jennings, M. Kent. "Partisan Commitment and Electoral Behavior in the Netherlands." (Unpublished, 1972).

Jennings, M. Kent, and Niemi, Richard G. "The Transmission of Political Values from Parent to Child." *American Political Science Review* 62 (March 1968): 168–84.

Jensen, Richard. *The Winning of the Midwest: Social and Political Conflict, 1888–1896.* Chicago: University of Chicago Press, 1971.

Johnson, Chalmers. *Revolutionary Change.* Boston: Little, Brown & Co., 1966.

Kelley, Stanley, Jr.; Ayres, Richard; and Bower, William J. "Registration and Voting: Putting First Things First." *American Political Science Review* 61 (June 1967): 359–77.

Key, V. O., Jr. *The Responsible Electorate.* New York: Random House, 1966.

———. "Secular Realignment and the Party System." *Journal of Politics* 21 (1959): 198–210.

———. "A Theory of Critical Elections." *Journal of Politics* 17 (February 1955): 3–18.

Key, V. O., and Munger, F. "Social Determinism and Electoral Decision: The Case of Indiana." In *American Voting Behavior,* edited by E. Burdick and A. J. Brodbeck, pp. 281–307. Glencoe: Free Press, 1959.

Kim, Jae-On; Petrocik, John R.; and Enokson, Stephen N. "Voter Turnout among the American States: Systemic and Individual Components." *American Political Science Review* 69 (March 1975): 107–30.

Klecka, William R. "Applying Political Generations to the Study of Political Behavior." *Public Opinion Quarterly* 35 (Fall 1971): 358–73.

Kleppner, Paul. *The Cross of Culture: A Social Analysis of Midwestern Politics 1850–1900.* New York: Free Press, 1970.

Ladd, Everett C., Jr. *American Political Parties: Social Change and Political Response.* New York: W. W. Norton, 1970.

Ladd, Everett C., Jr., and Hadley, Charles. *Transformations of the American Party System.* New York: W. W. Norton, 1975.

Lichtman, Allan J. "Critical Election Theory and the Reality of American Presidential Politics, 1916–1940." *American Historical Review* 81 (April 1976): 317–50.

Lijphart, Arend. *The Politics of Accommodation: Pluralism and Democracy in the Netherlands.* Berkeley: University of California Press, 1968.

Lipset, S. M. *Agrarian Socialism.* Garden City, N.Y.: Doubleday, 1968.

————. *Political Man.* Garden City, N.Y.: Doubleday, 1960.

Lipset, S. M., and Rokkan, Stein. *Party Systems and Voter Alignments.* New York: Free Press, 1967.

Lubell, Samuel. *The Future of American Politics.* New York: Harper, 1951.

Maccoby, Eleanor E.; Matthews, Richard E.; and Morton, Anton S. "Youth and Political Change." *Public Opinion Quarterly* 18 (Spring 1954): 23–29.

McPhee, William, and Ferguson, Jack. "Political Immunization." In *Public Opinion and Congressional Elections*, edited by William McPhee and Nathan Glaser, pp. 155–79. New York: Free Press, 1962.

MacRae, Duncan, and Meldrum, James A. "Critical Elections in Illinois: 1888–1958." *American Political Science Review* 54 (September 1960): 667–83.

McSeveney, Samuel. *The Politics of Depression: Political Behavior in the Northeast, 1893–1896.* New York: Oxford University Press, 1972.

Mannheim, Karl. "The Problem of Generations." In *Essays on the Sociology of Knowledge*, edited by Paul Kecskemeti, pp. 276–322. London: Routledge & Kegan Paul, 1952.

Merriam, Charles. *Chicago: A More Intimate View of Urban Politics.* New York: Macmillan Co., 1929.

Merriam, Charles E., and Gosnell, H. F. *Nonvoting.* Chicago: University of Chicago Press, 1924.

Nie, Norman H.; Verba, Sidney; and Petrocik, John R. *The Changing American Voter.* Cambridge: Harvard University Press, 1976.

Petrocik, John R. "Changing Party Coalitions and the Attitudinal Basis of Realignment: 1952–1972." Ph.D. thesis, University of Chicago, 1975.

Phillips, Kevin. *The Emerging Republican Majority*. New York: Arlington House, 1968.

Pomper, Gerald M. "Classification of Presidential Elections." *Journal of Politics* 29 (1967): 535–66.

————. "From Confusion to Clarity: Issues and American Voters, 1956–1968." *American Political Science Review* 66 (June 1972): 415–28.

Price, Douglas. "Critical Elections and Party History: A Critical View." *Polity* 4 (Winter 1971): 236.

Prindle, David. "Mobilization and Realignment in Pittsburgh, 1920–1940." (Unpublished, 1975).

Przeworski, Adam. "Institutionalization of Voting Patterns, or Is Mobilization the Source of Decay?" *American Political Science Review* 69 (March 1975): 49–67.

Public Service Leader, Chicago (1920–40).

Robinson, E. E. *They Voted for Roosevelt*. New York: Octagon Books, 1970.

Robinson, W. S. "Ecological Correlations and the Behavior of Individuals." *American Sociological Review* 15 (1950): 351–57.

Rose, Richard, and Urwin, Derek. "Persistence and Change in Western Party Systems since 1945." *Political Studies* 18 (Summer 1970): 287–319.

————. "Social Cohesion, Political Parties and Strains on Regimes." *Canadian Political Studies* 2 (April 1969): 1–67.

Royko, Mike. *Boss: Richard J. Daley of Chicago*. New York: Dutton, 1972.

Ryder, Norman B. "The Cohort as a Concept in the Study of Social Change." *American Sociological Review* 30 (December 1965): 843–61.

Sani, Giacomo. "Electoral Change in Italy." (Unpublished, 1976).

————. "Secular Trends and Party Realignments in Italy: The 1975 Election." Paper presented at the American Political Science Association meeting, 1975.

Scammon, Richard M., and Wattenberg, Ben J. *The Real Majority*. New York: Coward, McCann & Geoghegan, 1970.

Schattschneider, E. E. *The Semi-Sovereign People*. New York: Holt, Rinehart & Winston, 1960.

Segal, David, et al. "Mortality and Political Partisanship: A Test of the Butler-Stokes Hypothesis." *Comparative Politics* 4 (July 1973): 601–10.

Sellers, Charles. "The Equilibrium Cycle in Two-Party Politics." *Public Opinion Quarterly* 29 (1965): 16–38.

Shively, W. Phillips. " 'Ecological' Inference: The Use of Aggregate Data to Study Individuals." *American Political Science Review* 63 (December 1969): 1183–96.

———. "A Reinterpretation of the New Deal Realignment." *Public Opinion Quarterly* 35 (1971–72): 620–24.

Shover, John L. "The Emergence of a Two-Party System in Republican Philadelphia, 1924–1936." *Journal of Interdisciplinary History* 60 (1974): 1000–1002.

———. "Was 1928 a Critical Election in California?" In *Electoral Change and Stability in American Political History*, edited by Jerome M. Clubb and Howard W. Allen, pp. 215–34. New York: Free Press, 1971.

Stave, Bruce M. *The New Deal and the Last Hurrah*. Pittsburgh: University of Pittsburgh Press, 1970.

Sundquist, James L. *Dynamics of the Party System*. Washington, D.C.: Brookings Institution, 1973.

Taeuber, I. B., and Taeuber, C. *People of the United States*. Washington, D.C.: Bureau of the Census, 1971.

Thurner, Arthur W. "The Impact of Ethnic Groups on the Democratic Party in Chicago 1920–1928." Ph.D. diss., University of Chicago, 1966.

Tingsten, Herbert. *Political Behavior*. London: King, 1937.

U.S. Department of Commerce, Bureau of the Census. *Fifteenth Census of the United States: 1930*. Washington, D.C.: Government Printing Office.

———. *Sixteenth Census of the United States: 1940*. Washington, D.C.: Government Printing Office.

———. *Religious Bodies*, vol. 1. Washington, D.C.: Government Printing Office, 1936.

Statistical Abstract of the United States: 1975. Washington, D.C.: Government Printing Office, 1975.

Weir, Blair T. "The Distortion of Voter Recall." *American Journal of Political Science* 79 (February 1975): 53–62.

Williamson, Chilton. *American Suffrage from Property to Democracy, 1760–1870*. Princeton, N.J.: Princeton University Press, 1960.

Index